T0227910

THE INFLUENTIAL PROJECT MANAGER

Winning Over Team Members
and Stakeholders

Best Practices and Advances in Program Management Series

Series Editor
Ginger Levin

THE INFLUENTIAL PROJECT MANAGER

Winning Over Team Members and Stakeholders

ALFONSO BUCERO

CRC Press
Taylor & Francis Group
Boca Raton London New York

CRC Press is an imprint of the
Taylor & Francis Group, an **informa** business
AN AUERBACH BOOK

CRC Press
Taylor & Francis Group
6000 Broken Sound Parkway NW, Suite 300
Boca Raton, FL 33487-2742

© 2015 by Taylor & Francis Group, LLC
CRC Press is an imprint of Taylor & Francis Group, an Informa business

No claim to original U.S. Government works

Version Date: 20140626

ISBN-13: 978-1-4665-9633-7 (pbk)
ISBN-13: 978-1-138-44032-6 (hbk)

This book contains information obtained from authentic and highly regarded sources. Reasonable efforts have been made to publish reliable data and information, but the author and publisher cannot assume responsibility for the validity of all materials or the consequences of their use. The authors and publishers have attempted to trace the copyright holders of all material reproduced in this publication and apologize to copyright holders if permission to publish in this form has not been obtained. If any copyright material has not been acknowledged please write and let us know so we may rectify in any future reprint.

Except as permitted under U.S. Copyright Law, no part of this book may be reprinted, reproduced, transmitted, or utilized in any form by any electronic, mechanical, or other means, now known or hereafter invented, including photocopying, microfilming, and recording, or in any information storage or retrieval system, without written permission from the publishers.

For permission to photocopy or use material electronically from this work, please access www.copyright.com (http://www.copyright.com/) or contact the Copyright Clearance Center, Inc. (CCC), 222 Rosewood Drive, Danvers, MA 01923, 978-750-8400. CCC is a not-for-profit organization that provides licenses and registration for a variety of users. For organizations that have been granted a photocopy license by the CCC, a separate system of payment has been arranged.

Trademark Notice: Product or corporate names may be trademarks or registered trademarks, and are used only for identification and explanation without intent to infringe.

Library of Congress Cataloging-in-Publication Data

Bucero, Alfonso, 1956-
     The influential project manager : winning over team members and stakeholders / Alfonso Bucero.
          pages cm. -- (Best practices and advances in program management series)
     Includes bibliographical references and index.
     ISBN 978-1-4665-9633-7 (paperback)
     1. Project management. 2. Teams in the workplace--Management. I. Title.

HD69.P75B776 2015
658.4'04--dc23   2014022710

Visit the Taylor & Francis Web site at
http://www.taylorandfrancis.com

and the CRC Press Web site at
http://www.crcpress.com

This book is dedicated to three different project influencers:

All upper managers, executives, and project managers who helped me directly or indirectly to make this project happen, contributing their opinions, experiences, and real practices.

To Taylor & Francis editors who sponsored me on this project, offering their commitment and support from the start to the end of this project.

To my wife, Rose, who always supported and encouraged me to get this project finished.

Contents

PART III   RIDE YOUR HORSE

About the Author

Alfonso Bucero, MSc, PMP, PMI-RMP, PMI Fellow, is the founder and managing partner of BUCERO PM Consulting (www.abucero. com). He managed IIL Spain for almost two years, and he was a senior project manager at Hewlett-Packard Spain (Madrid Office) for more than thirteen years.

Bucero is a member of the Project Management Institute (PMI), ALI (Asociación de Licenciados, Ingenieros y Doctores en Informática) and AEIPRO (IPMA member). Bucero was the founder, sponsor, and president of PMI Barcelona, Spain Chapter, and he is an IPMA Assessor. He was a member of the Congress Project Action Team of PMI EMEA's Congresses in Edinburgh (2005), Madrid (2006), and Budapest (2007). He graduated from PMI's Leadership Institute Master Class 2007 in Atlanta at the PMI NA Global Congress. He was president of the PMI Madrid Spain Chapter for two years and has served as Component Mentor for Region 8 Southwest since 2011. He received the PMI Distinguished Contribution Award in 2010 for his long and varied body of work, and the PMI Fellow Award in 2011 from the PMI for his sustained contribution to the development of the profession internationally.

Bucero has a computer science engineering degree from Universidad Politecnica (Madrid), and is a PhD candidate in project management at the University of Mondragon in Spain. He has 31 years of practical experience and 25 of them in project management worldwide. He has managed and consulted on projects in various countries across Europe.

Since 1992, Bucero has been a frequent speaker at international PMI Congresses, IPMA Congresses, and PMI SeminarsWorld. He has been a keynote speaker in several congresses worldwide. He delivers project management training and consulting services in several countries worldwide. As a "project management believer," he defends passion, persistence, and patience as vital keys for project success. Bucero has been a professor for MEDIP (Master in Construction and Project Management) at the Universidad Politecnica since 2004, and he is a professor and executive consultant for the Marketing & Finance Business School in Bilbao (Spain).

He authored the book *Dirección de Proyectos, Una Nueva Vision* published by LITO GRAPO Editors (2003). He contributed a chapter to *Creating the Project Office* published by Jossey-Bass (2004), authored by Randall L. Englund, Robert J. Graham, and Paul Dinsmore. Bucero coauthored with Randall L. Englund the book *Project Sponsorship* published by Jossey-Bass (2006). He authored the book *Today Is a Good Day: Attitudes for Achieving Project Success*, published by Multimedia Publishing in Canada (2010). Bucero contributed the chapter "From Commander to Sponsor: Building Executive Support for Project Success" in the book *Advising Upwards* (2011) authored by Lynda Bourne in Australia. He also contributed a chapter to the book *Project Management circa 2025* edited by Dr. David I. Cleland and Dr. Bopaya Bidanda in 2010.

Bucero also coauthored with Randall L. Englund the books *The Complete Project Manager* and *The Complete Project Manager Toolkit* published by Management Concepts on March 2012, and published a new version of his book *Dirección de Proyectos, Una Nueva Vision*, and the book *Hoy Es un Buen Día* (Spanish translation of *Today Is a Good Day*). He has also contributed to professional magazines in the United States, Russia (SOVNET), India (ICFAI), Argentina, and Spain. Bucero was a contributing editor for six years for the "Crossing Borders" column of *PM Network* magazine, published by the PMI. He is a monthly contributor for the Project Connections Blog, and has published several project management articles in other magazines.

You can reach Alfonso Bucero at alfonso.bucero@abucero.com.

Introduction

The first question that came to my mind when I decided to write this book was: Why write a book about influence? I believe influence is a key skill a project manager must develop. Over the years, I have managed different projects and without being conscious of it, I indirectly influenced many people through my behavior, actions, and decisions.

Persuading people to help meet project goals was a difficult task for me when I started as a project management practitioner. Some years later, I understood that everyone has influence on other people. It does not matter who you are or what your job is. You don't have to be in a high-profile job to be a person of influence. In fact, if your life in any way connects with other people, you can influence these people. Everything you do in your job, at home, and with your colleagues and friends has an impact on the lives of the people around you.

You, as a project manager, influence all your project stakeholders. In fact, if you want to be successful as a project manager or to make a positive impact on your projects, you need to become a person of influence. Without influence, there can be no success. For example, if you are a project manager your success depends on your ability to positively influence your team members. No matter what your professional or personal goals are in life, or what you want to accomplish, you can achieve them faster, you can be more effective, and the contribution you make can last longer if you learn how to become a person of influence.

It is well known that many project managers do not have authority, but nevertheless they need to have influence to achieve project success. Influence is invisible because it is about how people think. We cannot see people's thoughts. Thoughts drive behavior, which drives actions and results. We can look at the results that influential project managers achieve but still have no idea about what makes them influential. Just as we cannot understand a person by looking at his/her shadow, we cannot understand influence by looking at its effect. We have to look for the causes of influence, not at its effects.

In my opinion, *thinking* like an influencer is the first and most important step to becoming an influential project manager. We do not need to sell our soul or clone our brain to become influential. We do not need to become someone else. We simply need to build on the best of who we already are.

Your Influence Is Not the Same with All People

I have observed that influence is very curious. Even though we can affect almost everyone around us, our level of influence is not the same with everyone. For example, when you have a meeting with your team members and you present an idea to them or make a suggestion, do they all respond in the same way? Of course not. One person may think all your ideas are inspired. Another may view everything you say with skepticism. You can identify which one you have influence with. On the other hand, the skeptic who resisted your idea may be more accepting if an executive presented it.

If you pay attention to people's responses to yourself and others, you can see that people respond to one another according to their level of influence. I consider influence like a specific application of influence. Influence does not come to us instantaneously; it grows by stages.

We are influenced by what we see. For instance, when my children were young no matter what I told them to do, their natural inclination was to imitate my behavior. Now they are adults and that does not happen anymore. Perhaps because when people are grown they do not need somebody with authority to move forward, that is, they do not need the father's authority. For most people, if they believe that you are positive and trustworthy and have admirable qualities, they will seek you as an influencer in their lives. And the better they get to know you, the greater your credibility will be and the higher your influence can become if they like what they see. For example, when I deliver training sessions and workshops and I promise to share some information (e.g., exercises, templates, and examples) with the workshop attendees, after the workshop I send the promised information to them.

If you were to attend Project Management Institute (PMI) congresses, the people you meet there do not know you, and at first you have no influence with them at all. If someone they trust introduces you to them and gives you an endorsement, you can temporarily "borrow" some of that person's influence. It happened to me many years ago; let me share with you my story. I had published my first article in *PM Network* in 2002. It happened because Randall L. Englund, my best friend, who is an executive consultant, speaker, and author, lent me his influence when he introduced me to *PM Network* editor Ross Foti. Englund had a very good reputation as a book author. He had written several articles for *PM Network* and other magazines, and he is the author of five books in the project management field. Obviously I needed to get some columns published until I was recognized. People will assume that you are credible until they know you better. But as soon as they have some time to observe you, you either build or bust that influence by your actions. Some people are very influenced by the image a well-known person has because of the actions and attitudes they believe that person represents.

If you want to make a really significant impact on the lives of other people, you have to do it up close. And that brings you to the second level of influence: *motivating*. You motivate people when you encourage them and communicate with them on an emotional level. The process creates a bridge between you and them, and builds their confidence and sense of self-worth. For instance, I always encourage people at professional congresses to participate and present their experiences in front of others. I always tell people about my experience presenting my first paper on project management at an international congress and how the reaction of the attendees encouraged me to continue presenting.

I consider *mentoring* the third level of influence. That means listening to people's needs and problems. You probably will not be able to solve their problems immediately but at least you can share similar experiences with them. Being positive is crucial. I am lucky because I have acted as a PMI mentor in the past, and I had experienced the issues and conflicts that arise in professional associations. The key is how to be an active listener. If you want to influence your mentees, then you need to effectively listen to them. Stop thinking and listen to them first, second, understand the issue or problem, third, think about alternatives, and finally, try to negotiate solutions.

The fourth level of influence is *multiplying*. The highest level of influence you can have in others' lives is the multiplication level. As a multiplying influencer, you help people you are influencing to become positive influencers in the lives of others, and pass on not only what they have received from you but also what they have learned and gleaned on their own. Few people ever make it to this influence level, but everyone has the potential to do so. You can be a model to the masses, but to go the higher levels of influence, you have to work with individuals. What you say and, more important, what you do are a model for those who follow you.

Positive influencers give value to other people. I don't know what kind of influence you have on others today as you read this book. Your actions may touch the lives of hundreds of people, or perhaps you may influence two or three team members or colleagues. The number of people is not what is most important. The key point is to remember that your level of influence is not static. Even if you have had a negative effect on others in the past, you can turn that around and make your impact a positive one. I want to help you become a project manager of high influence. You can have an incredibly positive impact on the lives of others. You can give a lot of value to them.

I don't know exactly what your dream is in life or what kind of legacy you want to leave. But if you want to make an impact, you will have to become a person capable of influencing others. As a project manager your destiny is learning from your mistakes when managing projects. My best advice for gaining influence is to know people more and more, learn from their reactions, and step by step you will learn about their reactions and you will be better prepared to influence them.

The Horse Story

For several years I have been telling my horse joke every time I need to convince somebody about the power of one's project management beliefs. Only when you believe in something can you sell it. I use this joke with my customers, colleagues, and peers. I try to give others my passion in telling the joke and I think I have shared it many times. However, I was not conscious about how I was influencing people when using that story over the years.

Many people remember me because of that joke; I think that means that I was able to influence them in some way. But let me tell it.

Let's imagine a gypsy who wants to sell a horse, and the gypsy says to a man: "I want to sell you a horse."

The man answers him: "I don't need any horse."

"Oh yes, you need it," says the gypsy. "You have some children and a wife. This horse wakes up very early in the morning, does all the housework, goes to the supermarket to do your shopping, and when you come back in the evening the meals are cooked. This is a fantastic horse. You need to buy it."

The man says: "I don't believe you, but I'll buy that horse."

Two months later the gypsy and the man meet each other again, and the man says to the gypsy: "That is an awful horse. It bothers my neighbors at 3:00 a.m. It kicks my children every day. I hate that horse. Please take away that horse."

The gypsy man smiles and says, "Continue talking about the horse that way and you will not be able to sell it again."

When I analyzed my story over the years, I discovered that I was influencing project managers' and executives' behaviors in my talks and presentations. Although the horse story is an example of persuasion, I always use it to demonstrate to project managers that they need to believe in their projects to be able to get the buy-in from executives. Every project is a "horse" you need to believe in, because if not, you cannot sell it to your customer or to the rest of the project stakeholders.

Persuasion consists of moving other people to voluntarily accept your point of view. Influence is the ability to exert power on somebody else. People who influence do not want to change attitudes, but people who persuade try to change them. I have become well known worldwide because of my positive attitude managing projects. What I learned is that every one of us influences people every day, but we are often not conscious of it. Remember, if you want to influence people, if you want to sell an idea or proposal to somebody, you need to prepare yourself (and the horse) if you want to be able to sell it.

Definitions

There are several definitions of influence. One is a power affecting a person, thing, or course of events, especially a power that operates without any direct or apparent effort. Influence may be also defined as the power to sway or affect based on prestige, wealth, ability, or position. Another definition is a determining factor, such as the positions of the stars and planets at the time of one's birth, which many believe affects an individual's tendencies and characteristics. A project manager needs to achieve results by influencing team members and stakeholders, and needs to develop that skill to be successful.

Influence versus Persuasion

Is the gypsy a persuader or an influencer? Persuasion is important but dangerous. If you persuade someone the wrong way, you lose influence. If the gypsy tries to sell a bad horse, he will lose his influence. We have all been victims of salespeople, colleagues, or bosses who use great persuasion techniques to make us do something we later regret. (Such as buying a horse that does housework!) And next time we see that person, we know not to trust him. The gypsy, despite being less than trustworthy, still teaches a valuable lesson and that ultimately has influence. This book shows how you can persuade and build influence at the same time. Instead of avoiding you, people will want to work with you more. But you must persuade them the right way.

Influencers play for much higher stakes than persuaders. Influencers do not want to be successful only one time. They want to build commitment that lasts. This means that influencers think and act very differently from persuaders. Persuaders start and finish with their own needs. They want to sell their product or plant their idea in another person's head. Communication tends to be one way: Persuaders do most of the talking as they extol the virtues of the product or idea they want to push. Influencers still have goals to achieve but think differently about how to get there. They see the world through other people's eyes, and adapt their message and behavior accordingly. The ideal outcome is not simply to persuade someone; it is to build an alliance of mutual trust and respect. Achieving this takes a lot of time, effort, and skill. But it is a great investment that yields rich dividends over a long period. What are the differences between influence and persuasion? See Table I.1.

Persuasion is the here-and-now skill we have to learn. Influence is our investment in the future. As a project manager regularly dealing with people, it pays to learn influence and persuasion.

Table I.1 Characteristics of Persuasion versus Influence

PERSUASION CHARACTERISTICS	INFLUENCE CHARACTERISTICS
Transactional	Creating and maintaining a relationship
Win–lose	Win–win situation
Competitive	Collaborative
One-off event	Permanent
Zero-sum game	One plus one equals two
Short-term goals	Long-term goals
Me versus you	"We" instead of "I"
See my needs only	See each other's needs
Kills trust	Builds trust

Basics of Influence

I would like to share with you four ways of influential thinking for project managers (Figure I.1): be ambitious, walk in other people's shoes, develop commitment, and start at the end.

1. Be ambitious—Lack of ambition is a recipe for a quiet life in the backwaters of underachievement. For many project managers, the greatest barrier to success is in their heads. They accept low expectations for themselves. Low expectations are always self-fulfilling. Ambitious project managers have high expectations of themselves and others. They reach for the stars. Even if they fail and only reach the moon, they will be far ahead of others whose expectations reach no further than next year's beach vacation. Unambitious project managers have never changed the world. Ambitious people are not satisfied with the status quo. They want to change things and make things happen.

   Ambition that is all "me, me, me" is not influential. It leads to conflict and fails to build networks of trust and support among your team and other project stakeholders. Ambition that is "we, we, we" is influential. It stretches people and teams, and builds commitment and camaraderie. The mindset of ambition is focused on opportunity and positive attitude.

2. Walk in other people's shoes—I have seen some project managers who think they are the center of the universe. Influencers may also think that they are the center of the universe, but they do not always show it. So you need to work hard to see

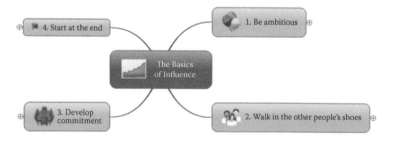

Figure I.1   Basics.

the world through the eyes of each person you want to influence. As a project manager I was always asking myself difficult questions:

a. Why should this person want to talk to me?

b. Why should this person want to follow or support me?

c. What does he or she want? What does he or she not want?
    How can I use that to my advantage?

d. How can I find out more about this person?

e. What other choices do I have? Why should he prefer my
    way?

Walking in other people's shoes is not about being nice to
other people or even agreeing with them. It is about understanding them. Once we understand someone we can start to
play his/her tune. The core skill for walking in other people's
shoes is very simple: listen to them but listen actively.

3. Develop commitment—Commitment is a mind-set central to
    the world of influence, not control. A control mind-set likes
    hierarchy: power comes from position. This makes it very limit-
    ing: the control mind-set does not reach beyond the barriers of
    the hierarchy to make things happen outside a limited range of
    control. The controlling mind-set is enabled by the organiza-
    tion but also limited by it. The controlling mind-set thinks that
    commitment is a one-way street: anyone lower in the organiza-
    tion must show commitment to people higher in the organiza-
    tion. Teamwork for a controlling manager means "my way or no
    way": if you do not obey, then you are not a good team player.

    A commitment mind-set is not constrained by hierarchy
    or by the formal limitations of power. It builds a network
    of informal alliances that enables an influencer to achieve
    things far beyond the dreams of the controlling mind-set.
    Commitment is a two-way street based on mutual obliga-
    tions. Building commitment takes time and skill. Influencers
    do not expect to build trustful partnerships overnight. These
    things take time. But once built, such partnerships can pay
    dividends for a lifetime.

4. Start at the end—Influential people start at the end. They
    work out the desired goal and then work back from there.
    They map the journey from the destination back to today. If

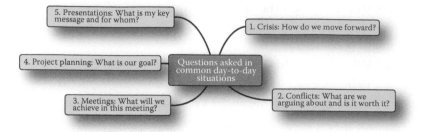

Figure I.2 Day to day.

we start from where we are, we may decide that our goal is not achievable. If we start at the end, the only question we should ask is, "How do we get there?" not "Can we get there?"

Starting at the end is a mind-set that consistently drives more effective behavior. It is focused on the future rather than the past, on action rather than analysis, and on outcome rather than on process. This mind-set in Figure I.2 shows some of the questions asked in common day-to-day situations:

- Crisis: "How do we move forward?" not "What went wrong and who can I blame?"
- Conflicts: "What are we arguing about and is it worth it?" not "How do I win?"
- Meetings: "What will we achieve in this meeting?" not "What is the formal agenda?"
- Project planning: "What is our goal?" not "What is the process and where is the risk log?"
- Presentations: "What is my key message and for whom?" not "Can we prepare another 50 PowerPoint slides, just in case we get a question?

Starting at the end requires firmness about the goals but flexibility about the means. This flexibility makes it much easier to adapt to other people and to build commitment. People who can act only in control mode lack such flexibility; they hope that strict compliance with a process will yield the right outcome. They use the same map, whatever their journey may be. However hard they run, they never make progress; they simply cover the same course faster. Starting at the end ensures an influencer chooses a worthwhile destination.

Learn How to Influence and Persuade

I never found any recipe that allows you to create a magic potion called influence and persuasion. Instead, you can learn a range of skills and techniques. You do not have to learn them all at once. My best practice is to try one skill at a time. Each skill can make you a better influencer and a better persuader. Learn all of them, and you can acquire a sort of magic by which people are more willing to follow you. This book is a guide for you. I learned from experience more than anything else. So this book is the help you need to guide your experiences. It is written for practicing project managers and executives who need to cope with the daily reality of dealing with difficult team members, colleagues, executives, and other project stakeholders.

Each skill is mastered through continual trial and error. I illustrate both the failures and successes. The failures are important because readers can learn from them. If you can avoid the many pitfalls I fell into in the course of working on this book, then that will save you considerable pain. Each skill is illustrated with real-life examples. The good news is that you do not have to follow a script to be influential or persuasive. You can be yourself with your own unique style. But behind that style is a rigorous set of skills, structures, and ways of thinking that enable you to succeed.

Failing at Persuasion

In my experience with project managers I saw some project managers failing at persuasion. Some of the common mistakes they made are as follows:

1. *They attempt to make their case up front with a hard sell.* Project managers strongly state their position at the outset, and then through a process of persistence, logic, and exuberance, they try to push the idea to a close. In reality, setting out a strong position at the start of a persuasion effort gives potential opponents something to grab on to—and fight against. In my opinion, effective persuaders do not begin the process by giving their colleagues a clear target to attack.
2. *They resist compromise.* Too many project managers see compromise as surrender, but it is essential to constructive

persuasion. Before people buy into a proposal, they want to see that the persuader is flexible enough to respond to their concerns. Compromises can often lead to better, more sustainable solutions. By not compromising, ineffective persuaders unconsciously send the message that they think persuasion is a one-way street. But persuasion is a process of give and take. To meaningfully persuade, we need not only to listen to others but also incorporate their perspectives into our own.

3. *They think the secret of persuasion lies in presenting great arguments.* In persuading people to change their minds, great arguments matter. No doubt about it. But arguments, per se, are only one part of the equation. Other factors matter just as much, such as the persuader's credibility and ability to create a mutually beneficial proposition, as well as connecting on the right emotional level with an audience and communicating through vivid language that makes arguments come alive.

4. *They assume persuasion is a one-shot effort.* Persuasion is a process not an event. Rarely, if ever, is it possible to arrive at a shared solution on the first try. More often than not, persuasion involves listening to people, testing a position, and developing a new position that reflects input from the group. More testing, incorporating compromises, and then trying again. If this sounds like a slow and difficult process, that's because it is. But the results are worth the effort.

Book Structure

This book integrates different pieces to develop and sustain your influencing skills as a project manager.

Outline

Each chapter highlights thoughts and real stories about a particular subject linked to the influencing skill. Here is an outline of what is covered:

Part I: Training a Better Horse
Chapter 1: Ten Keys to Influence—When you try to sell something you need to convince others to support you and

your ideas. If you are successful on that, they will follow you willingly.

Chapter 2: Practice Active Listening—If you want to influence people, you need to listen to them first. So this chapter focuses on how to practice good listening and it gives you some tips and techniques to do that. A listening assessment tool is also provided in this chapter.

Chapter 3: Develop Trust—Trust is so central to our lives, but it should be earned. The most influential project managers tend to be the most trusted. People are prepared to work with people they trust. A trust assessment is also provided in this chapter.

Chapter 4: Practice Your Integrity—Learn how important it is to develop your integrity actions for project and organizational success. You need to practice your integrity if you want to influence people successfully.

Chapter 5: Influence to Win—The best way to win is without fighting; you do not need to spend energy that can be used to do positive things. A checklist to promote wins is provided at the end of this chapter.

Chapter 6: Practice Your Generosity—As generosity becomes scarcer, it becomes more valuable. You need to practice your generosity in order to influence people. Generosity is not a very common trait in most of project managers. Take care of it and cultivate it.

Chapter 7: Understanding People—Understanding people certainly impacts your ability to communicate with them. And communication is a key to influencing people. This chapter provides a practical checklist.

Chapter 8: Develop Commitment—When you make a commitment and are willing to do whatever it takes, you begin to attract people and circumstances necessary to accomplish your goal. Learn how to develop your commitment to influence people through what they see you do.

Chapter 9: Cultivate Your Informal Power—Learn how to procure informal power to be a good and successful influencer. Project managers need to use informal power to make things happen.

Throughout the book I will emphasize the importance of being positive and developing a positive attitude when trying to develop your influence skills as a project manager. All the best practices and ideas shared in this book are based on the experiences of myself and project management colleagues.

Summary

I hope this book influences you as a project manager, project practitioner, or executive, as well as a person. Read it carefully and try to do the checklists and exercises. If you finally have been influenced by this book, please lend your influence to somebody else. That person will be another person of influence.

We have made it through the first decade of the twenty-first century and still we are running into problems about how to influence our leaders to make necessary changes happen. Make a difference and develop your influence skills.

We have more and more challenging projects to manage and need better prepared people to lead and manage. If you achieve better influence skills, I'll be a happy contributor to your professional development. If you fail, please never give up. Cultivate a positive attitude and always look at the bright side of life.

Read this book chapter by chapter and try to test if the assessment and other tools provided are useful for your working life as a project manager. Finally, ask yourself which people have influenced you and reflect about their characteristics and patterns. I always learn a lot from observing how people act and react in different project scenarios and situations.

I encourage you to share with me your opinions, ideas, feedback, and real stories in order to improve future editions of this book. You may reach me at alfonso.bucero@abucero.com. All of you can be my teachers. Any mistake you may find in this book is my responsibility and only mine.

I thank Dr. Ginger Levin for her encouragement to write this book, and my best friend Randall L. Englund, who helped me with his feedback, comments, and advice.

Are you ready to move to the first chapter? Go ahead, read and enjoy. Today is a good day to start developing your influence skills.

PART I
TRAINING A BETTER HORSE

1

Ten Keys to Influence

The authentic leadership is in taking action, not in having, on influencing in the benefit of the project, not in manipulating for my own benefit.

Unknown

I hope you have already read my horse story. But please do not misunderstand me. I do not mean you need to lie to persuade people. Persuasion is the ability to convince people. The gypsy man wanted to convince the Spanish man about the great skills of the horse. When the Spanish man used the horse he found some lack of skills in it. So, my message is that when you want to sell a horse you need to get that horse prepared. The ability of selling a product or service is a must for the complete project manager (*The Complete Project Manager*, Randall L. Englund and A. Bucero, 2012, Management Concepts).

When you try to sell something you need to convince others to support you and your ideas, so you are trying to persuade them. If you do this well they will follow you willingly, not reluctantly; then you will influence them based on your behavior, on the way you do things. For years I did not understand that magic control salespeople usually have to persuade colleagues or customers to support or buy something. However, during my career as a project manager, I needed to talk to many different project stakeholders. The first method I used was to establish a dialogue with the people I wanted or needed to influence.

Dialogue

A persuasive conversation is not a random one. A persuasive conversation has a structure and a purpose. I have observed that every persuasive conversation has the same structure. You can use the same structure whether you are engaged in a two-minute conversation or a two-month conversation about some big initiative. Only you will know that you are using the structure. A persuasive conversation gains more than agreement; it also builds commitment. People will trust you more and want to work with you more. The structure I am talking about follows seven steps, and I have used one of the words of my professional motto "Passion, Persistence, and Patience." In this case I use the word *passion* as the principle to be used in a persuasive conversation. In this case PASSION is an acronym meaning:

1. Preparation
2. Alignment
3. Situation review
4. So, what's in it for me?
5. Imagination
6. Overcome objections and obstacles
7. Next steps

To show you how this structure works, let me give you an example: My project team has been working very hard during the whole week. We have not achieved our deadline, but people feel exhausted and I thought they all needed a break if they want to be productive the next day. I thought it was time to get them out of the office and go home early to relax. Let's use Figure 1.1 and PASSION to work through this example.

1. Preparation—Make sure the whole team is in the room. Check with a couple of them that they were as tired as they looked. Ask for their attention.

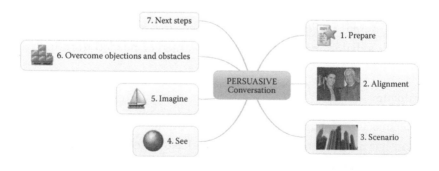

Figure 1.1   Persuasive conversations.

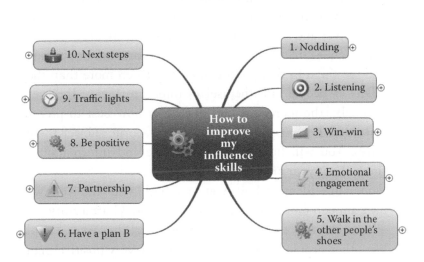

Figure 1.2   How to improve my influence skills.

2. Alignment—It has been a hard week, how are you all feeling? Many signals of discontent came by way of reply.
3. Situation—We are all tired, we need a break.
4. See—It is important to relax to have more strength the next day and be more productive.
5. Imagination—Let's go to the bar to see the tennis match.
6. Overcome objections and obstacles—I'll buy the first round.
7. Next steps—Last person out turns off the lights and buys the second round.

This persuasive conversation lasted a few minutes. Other conversations are not so easy, and take more time and persistence. That structure works for me. Initially it looks hard to use, but it is not. The more you use the structure, the better you will become. Please practice that when managing your team members in projects.

Based on my experience because I made a lot of mistakes during my professional career I want to share with you some principles that helped me to improve my influence skills. They are what I call the ten keys of influence (see Figure 1.2):

1. Nodding—In a conversation start the agreement process early. If they say something you disagree with, do not object

and start an argument. Ignore the comment. Focus on areas of agreement. You need to funnel the discussion toward your desired outcome. When you achieve an agreement, both parts are happier and have the feeling they are advancing.

2. Listening—Great persuaders have two ears and one mouth, and use them in that proportion. They listen more than they talk. Let people talk themselves into agreement. The more they talk, the more you find out about how best to present your idea. Let people talk about their favorite subject themselves. You will have much more time and information to think about your answer or reply.

3. Win–win—Identify how you can both win and you will have a much more productive conversation. Craft a story that allows the other person to show how smart they were. People like other people talking about them in a very positive manner, reinforcing their virtues and good skills.

4. Emotional engagement—It is easy to disagree with people you dislike, harder to argue against people you like. Use your empathy. If they annoy you, do not show it. Wear the mask of friendship. It needs to be rehearsed because it takes time because it is not natural, but it is possible. Practice, practice, and practice with that.

5. Walk in the other people's shoes—Do not try to batter people into submission with the brilliance of your idea or logic. You will simply annoy them and give them material to argue about. See how it looks from their side, what's in it for them, why they might object, and what you can do to prevent them objecting.

6. Have a plan B—Have a best outcome and be prepared to work backward from it. But always have a plan B. When you are sailing against the wind the quickest way forward is not a straight line; it is a zigzag. Learn to be flexible. If something may fail, it will fail for sure. Then you need to have other plan to react quickly enough to that failure.

7. Partnership—You are neither telling someone nor being told what to do. You are working together to discover a good outcome. This is especially important when dealing with important people. If you act as a junior, they will treat you as a

junior. Treat them not as a boss, but as a human being and as your partner in developing an idea or action.

8. Positivism—Be positive both in style and in substance. If you are not positive and enthusiastic about your idea, don't expect anyone else to be positive and enthusiastic for you (*Today Is a Good Day!*, Alfonso Bucero, Multi-Media Publications, 2010, Canada).

9. Traffic lights—Think of the conversation structure as a series of red traffic lights. Do not proceed to the next stage until the lights turn green. Do not get ahead of yourself; take your time and make sure each step is complete before moving to the next.

10. Next steps—Always have some next steps at the end of every conversation, otherwise the trail goes cold. Do not assume the other person is psychic; they will not know what the next steps are, so you have to suggest next steps to them.

Each of these influencing and persuading principles are explored in more detail in this book. If all you do is to apply some of these principles some of the time, you will find that you will become more persuasive and more influential.

Everyone has his/her own unique style and way of deploying the principles and structure of persuasion; it is not a mechanistic script that you have to read. To start, focus on one step (preparing the conversation) or any one of the ten principles you feel most comfortable with. With practice you can build up more steps and more principles. By way of consolidation, rest assured that even the most accomplished persuaders still mess up and are still learning after decades of experience. The goal is not perfection. The goal is improvement and learning.

Persuasive Conversations

Remember the hidden structure of the persuasive conversation has seven stages you need to pass through.

Preparation

Time spent preparing is rarely wasted. The preparation may take minutes or days as you prepare for a big meeting. Your preparation checklist should cover five basic questions:

1. What do I want to achieve in this meeting?
2. How will the other person see this issue?
   - What are their no-go areas?
   - What are their hot buttons? What will turn them on?
   - Why would they want to support this idea?
3. How should I interact with them? What is their style?
4. Are any logistics required for the meeting?
5. How will I start the meeting?

Preparation is crucial to success. You need to spend time thinking about the several scenarios you may find in your conversation.

Alignment

Alignment is where you need to start walking in the other person's shoes. You need to help them answer some questions that they will have in their heads:

- What is this discussion all about?
- Why should I talk to this person about this subject?
- Am I prepared to believe this person?
- Why am I talking now?

This part of the discussion starts "Hi Peter, how are you?" If Peter looks grumpy and harassed, it may be worth seeing what is chewing him up. If it is a bad time to talk, let Peter sort out his problems and set another time to meet.

At first meetings, alignment takes time and effort. The other person will be keen to know who you are and, bluntly, if it is worth talking to you. Making a formal pitch about your credentials may be necessary but can backfire. They may be unimpressed. Or they may dislike your boasting. Either way, it puts you in the position of a defendant and them in the position of judge and jury. The better way of doing this is to find some common background, for example, places you have worked, people you both know, conferences attended. These professional links are a chance to show that you know what you are talking about. Use the opportunity to flatter and soothe an executive ego. Even areas of social overlap, such as pastimes, build some mutual respect.

Once the other side is comfortable that they are talking to the right person at the right time, you can move explicitly to the main subject of discussion. For example: When managing a project for a savings bank in Spain (CGG), when we got to the bank the meeting started with the formal exchange of business cards. We quickly found we had many areas of common background and experience. They had identified some areas from our advance materials. It was a social chat that confirmed to them that we might know what we were talking about. Once they were relaxed we outlined how we wanted to run the meeting. This was the expectation that we had set, and they were happy to humor us. We made no presentation at all.

Situation Review

If you can both agree on the problem or opportunity, the chances are that the solution will be relatively easy to find. In many cases, persuasive conversations go wrong because the two sides have different views about what the problem or opportunity is. Invest time to agree explicitly on the problem. Even if you both agree on the problem in broad outline, the chances are that you will have different perspectives on it. Explore these perspectives. You do not need to persuade at this moment; you need to listen.

Remember to focus on their issue, opportunity, or problem, not on yours. Understand how they see the world before you try changing their view of the world. It is better to ask smart questions than to make smart comments. Smart questions are ones that get rich answers. Dumb questions get yes or no answers. Even if you get lucky with a yes, you have not learned anything about why they said yes. And if they say no, you hit a dead end. Smart/dumb comments are just that. They may be very smart and based on deep insight and knowledge, but they are also dumb because they invite a pointless argument. For example, see Table 1.1.

If the conversation later on goes wrong, come back to this point: Reaffirm what it is that you are trying to accomplish together. The situation review is the logical choke point of the conversation. If in doubt, always come back to this point to clarify and confirm.

Table 1.1   Situation Review

SMART QUESTIONS	DUMB QUESTIONS	SMART/DUMB COMMENTS
What are your priorities for the next year?	Is x your priority for the next year?	Our analysis shows that x, y, and z are your top priorities
How do your clients see this?	Do your clients like this?	Our research shows that your clients will love this.
What do you see as the major obstacles to progress?	Is this a major obstacle to success?	I know that this looks like a real obstacle, but it is not.
Why is this important to you?	Is this important to you?	Of course, everyone accepts that this is important and urgent.

So, What's in It for Me?

Now a huge bear trap opens up. It is tempting to leap to the solution and discuss how it works. If you do this, you will be speeding through several sets of red traffic lights. You may get lucky and survive, but you may well crash and burn. Take it easy. You are slowly building commitment; keep them nodding, keep them on your side.

Before they agree with your idea, they will have two questions rattling in the back of their minds:

- What are the benefits of your idea to me personally and to my organization?
- What are the risks to me personally and to my organization?

Your first talk is to explore the benefits of your idea. Leave the risks and problems until later. People buy solutions, not problems. If you focus on the problems too early, you will depress and discourage everyone and they will give up. They need the motivation of knowing what's in it for them and their organization.

Benefits are rational, emotional, and political. We normally focus on the rational benefits only, but humans are not computers. We have emotions. As social animals we also have politics. Be aware of all benefits and risks of your idea.

Rational benefits are obvious. Some are financials, others are not, but they have financial implications. Establish the financial impact of all of these benefits. Size the prize. If you are able to dangle a carrot worth millions in front of someone, then most people will start to show interest. The art is not to tell them this is worth millions.

Discuss it with them, produce the estimate together. If it is their estimate, they will believe it.

Political benefits and risks come down to a simple question: How will this affect me in my organization? No one wants to be the village idiot who backed a dumb idea or made a bad decision or negotiated poorly. You need to approach these issues crabwise: from the side. Diving overtly into the politics of your organization and your partner is unlikely to be productive. Instead, you can ask smart questions to reveal what the political landscape looks like:

- Who else needs to buy into this idea?
- How will they see this idea? What will they like about it? What risks will they see?
- How would you advise that we handle this issue when we see them?

When you frame the question this way, you give the other side the chance to air their personal fears under the guise of pretending that they are fears their colleagues have. Live with the deceit: It is a useful way of finding out what they really think.

Finally, you need to deal with the emotional aspects of your idea, which again come down to a simple question: What's in it for me (WIFM)? Once you understand what is in it for each person you are dealing with, you are on the high road to success. Or at least you can understand the real obstacles that lie on the road ahead.

The answer may be positive or negative. The problem with emotional objections is that no one talks about them. They disguise them with rational concerns such as that is too risky, it will cost too much, and health and safety will not allow it. And the more you argue about these rational objections, the more you ignore their real objection. Things get ugly fast.

Most WIFM objections come down to perceived risk in terms of success, workload, reputation, and so on. The key is to understand that risk is not absolute; it is relative. The default position of most people when faced with a risky idea is to kill it: doing nothing is less risky than doing something. So you have to change the balance of risk:

- Provide reassurance that the risks of your idea are modest and manageable.

- Show that the risks of doing nothing are real. Create the burning platform, find the bogeyman that will eat them up if they stand still.
- All of this takes time. Do not rush. Ask smart questions that lead them to the answer you want them to discover.

Your Idea

By this point, you are 90% of the way to success. Your client or colleague is ready to say yes. And yet you still have not actually proposed your idea. But your client and colleague now actively want to hear your solution: They agree on the problem, they see that there are big benefits in solving it, and any risks or objections are known and manageable. So all they want to know is how. At last, you are ready to tell them and they are ready to agree.

There are three ways of outlining your proposed idea.

Method 1—The simplest way is to tell them, in one sentence: "Let's start with an eight-week assessment with a small team, which will then lead to a focused effort over nine months to deliver the results you want."

You then move promptly to Stage 6 where you preempt and resolve any outstanding concerns they may have.

Method 2—Offer them a choice, so that they feel ownership over the course of action that they pick. Naturally, you will have a preferred solution and so you will want to make sure they pick the right one.

If you offer a choice, you change the terms of debate. You are no longer saying my way or no way. You set up a partnership discussion in which you are finding the best solution together. The simplest version of this is the three-choice trick:

- Choice A—Very big and exciting, but you know it is going to be too much and too risky.
- Choice B—This is the choice you prefer.
- Choice C—Low risk, low effort but really does not get anyone anywhere.

Let the other person tell you in no uncertain terms why A and C are useless choices. Let them confirm to themselves their wisdom, business judgment, and superiority. You can then profess your great thanks to them for guiding you to choice B, which you wanted all along.

Method 3—Ask your client or colleague to design the solution for you. In practice, you have to take them through a process of discovery so that they reveal to themselves the solution you have always wanted. This is more elaborate than the first two methods, but it is also more powerful. By letting someone come up with their own solution, you guarantee that they are genuinely committed to it. They can show off to others about how smart they were in figuring out the solution. Let them brag.

Overcome Objections and Obstacles: The Art of Persuasion

The best way to deal with problems and objections is to preempt them. If you have done your listening well in the early stages, you will know what the objections are likely to be, and you will be able to defuse them. For instance, if you know the budget will be an objection, you might mention in advance that the finance department has already looked at your idea. Even if they have not approved the idea, you can say that you are working with them to solve the problem.

Inevitably, there will be some objections. This is the "yes, but ..." part of the conversation. People start to say things like "Yes, but have you thought of ..." or "I agree, but how about ..." They are raising their anxieties and concerns. There are many ways of dealing with these concerns. Probably the worst way is to argue your case: the smarter you are, the more you will drive the other person into a corner. Argument simply generates more argument.

It is natural for us to react defensively to these objections: people are saying that they do not like our baby. The problem with a defensive reaction is that it simply provokes more argument. Soon enough both sides will be engaged in trench warfare to prove that they are right and the other side is wrong. The rational debate gets lost in the emotional need to be seen to be right.

So how can we define objections without fighting them? You use persuasion judo: use the force of their own argument to flatten their argument. There are three steps to persuasion:

1. Agree with the objection—This avoids the win–lose debate that results from a defensive reaction. The two of you are now in agreement and you face a common challenge. Here is the sort of language you can use:
   - "I agree. That has been worrying me."
   - "You're right. Other people have been raising the same issue."
2. Outline a potential solution in a way that does not put you on the line for defending the idea—For instance: "When I talked this through with other people, they came up with a range of solutions. One I liked in particular was …" You have just depersonalized the disagreement. If the solution is no good, then the other person is no longer arguing with you: they are arguing with an absent third party who suggested the idea. You are both on safe ground.
3. Ask for their advice—Ask if they have a better way of solving the challenge than the one you outlined. Again, the language can be simple: "Of course, that was just one idea. Would that work or do you have an even better way of dealing with it?"

So now you are getting your client or colleague to solve their own problem for you.

Next Steps

Never assume that you have agreement. Most managers are not great at telepathy. They will not know exactly what you want. Many people fall at this final hurdle. For instance, I was recently called in to see a government minister. I prepared thoroughly and it all went well. But I had been so focused on getting through the meeting that I had forgotten the most important thing of all. Government ministers have other things on their mind and do not have time to waste trying to work out what you are thinking or hoping for. You have to ask and be clear about what you want. Do not turn your golden opportunity into fool's gold.

Confirm your agreement. What you think has happened may not be the same as what the other person thinks has happened. There are four main ways of closing the conversation. In the first three cases you get positive confirmation that you both understand what you have agreed. Once you have agreement, follow up. The longer you leave it, the more the agreement will go cold and second thoughts will start coming up. If possible, make the agreement public; once committed in public, people find it hard to backtrack. Send an e-mail thanking them for their contribution and confirming the next steps. Ideally, give both parties a next step. You can show professionalism by following up. By asking for a next step from the other person, you reinforce your mutual agreement and their commitment.

Emotional Flow

The structure of your persuasive conversation is not just a rational framework. It is also an emotional framework (Table 1.2) in which you take someone on a journey from indifference or hostility to agreement and commitment. The traffic lights apply to each stage of the emotional journey as well as to the logic of your conversation. Here is how the structure of logic and emotion flow together. For the sake of simplicity I refer to the person you are persuading as a client, although they may be a colleague, supplier, regulator, vendor, partner, or anyone else.

Table 1.2 Emotional Flow

CONVERSATION STRUCTURE	LOGIC TRAFFIC LIGHTS	EMOTIONAL TRAFFIC LIGHTS
Preparation	You understand the client, have objectives, and have agreed on logistics	Client accepts need for meeting; expectations set
Alignment	You have confirmed the purpose of the meeting	Client feels comfortable talking to you; credibility and rapport established
Situation review	You understand the situation from the client's perspective	Client is now relaxed and confident that he or she has been heard and understood
So, what's in it for me?	You have established the "size of the prize"	Client is excited by the potential win to the organization and for self
Idea	You have stated your idea clearly and it is understood	Client confirms that he or she understands what you are asking for
Overcome objections and obstacles	Objections are understood, qualified, and resolved	Client is on your side, working to resolve any problems
Next steps	You agree on specific next steps with the client	Client expresses commitment to what happens next

The easiest way to see if the emotional traffic lights are green is to watch the body language. It is normally pretty obvious. If someone is leaning forward, smiling, talking warmly and positively, then you have green lights. If they are sitting back, arms folded, looking over your shoulder, looking at their smartphone, fidgeting, and giving short and tetchy answers to you, then it does not take a genius to work out that the emotional traffic lights are flashing bright red. When this happens, do not plow on. Go back to Stages 2 and 3, get some alignment and make sure you have understood what their perspective is.

By keeping this structure in your mind you can pace and direct the conversation as you see fit. You are not working to a script; you are not a pushy salesperson. You are being yourself. But you have a structure that gives direction and purpose to your conversation. Your conversation becomes persuasive and productive.

Classic Mistakes

Persuasive conversations rarely go wrong because the persuader does not have the right skills. They go wrong because the basics go wrong. Here, from hard-won experience, are some of the classics:

1. Persuading the wrong person—Do a brilliant job, gain agreement, and find the person you are talking to is not the real decision maker. The solution is to do your homework.
2. Leaving without next steps—This can happen even after a brilliant meeting where everything has gone well, but you forget to state exactly what happens next. It is then very awkward to go back a few days later and try to re-create the enthusiasm that existed before. And if things have not gone as planned, you always need a plan B, which should at least involve a follow-up conversation. Solution: know the outcome you want, and ask for it.
3. Falling in love with your own idea—You talk too much and talk over the other person who will not love your baby as much as you do. In fact, they may just see a noisy mess and will object to your baby. Listening is better than talking. Solution: ask smart questions, don't make smart comments. Failing that, buy duct tape and put it over your mouth.

4. Becoming defensive—When people object to your idea, it is easy to start arguing back. Then you just have an argument. It is better to win a friend than to win an argument. Solution: agree with the objection. Let them talk about their concerns. Ask them for advice on how they would solve their concern. Often the will solve their own problem.

5. Not following up—When you have an agreement, you need to reinforce it and confirm it. Otherwise, nothing will happen. Solution: send an e-mail immediately after the meeting thanking them for their great help and summarizing the main conclusions and next steps.

6. Having only one plan—This is fine when things go well. But we have to deal with human nature. The unexpected happens. You need to prepare for all eventualities and to be flexible. Solution: have a plan B, have an alternative.

7. Hiding behind PowerPoint—That tool is a disaster for persuaders. It makes you talk, not listen. It gives you no flexibility. It puts the other person in the role of judge and jury that is a role they will enjoy more than you, because you are the defendant they are judging.

Summary

The invisible structure behind the persuasive conversation has seven steps. Those steps match with part of my motto: Passion, persistence, and patience.

PASSION is the first one you need to apply:

1. Preparation
2. Alignment
3. Situation review
4. So, what's in it for me?
5. Imagination
6. Overcome objections and obstacles
7. Next steps

Apply this structure consistently and your discussions become cooperative, negative outcomes become positive, and passive agreements become active support.

The persuasive conversation, like most influencing skills, is most effective when it is invisible. People do not need to feel that they are being persuaded or influenced. Gently guide them in the right direction. Let them discover the right answer. Done well, they will think it is their own idea. They will commit willingly to the idea, whereas active persuading often leads to no more than passive and grudging agreement. Influencers go beyond that to build active and lasting support.

I do not consider myself as an excellent influencer, so I designed a questionnaire to evaluate my influence skills over the years. It is not a panacea but at least I hope it will help you to increase your focus on the aspects you can improve, because you can be a better influencer. Please repeat every day: I can be a better influencer.

Then please go to influence assessment in the next section and try to score the questions listed in the assessment. I suggest you do it honestly, and take enough time before answering. You need to reflect if your answers are the real truth or at least what you believe it is.

After scoring yourself please review the table with the suggestions about your scoring.

Influence Assessment

In the following assessment, please score yourself from 1 to 5 (1 is the minimum and 5 is the maximum).

QUESTION	SCORING (1–5)
1. Are you getting things done?	_____
2. Are other people seeking you out for advice to accomplish the most essential tasks and to make important decisions?	_____
3. Are you able to create alliances across business units, developing support?	_____
4. Do your credibility and respect as a project manager get people to embrace your ideas and want to be part of what you are doing?	_____
5. Do you have allies who support your ideas and help you accomplish the tasks that are deemed important?	_____
6. Do you sway decisions to your desired state because when you speak, people listen to what you have to say?	_____
7. Do people know they can depend on you to influence decisions and change outcomes for the better?	_____
8. Have you established mutual respect with people above you who want to hear and seek out your opinions, ideas, and insights?	_____

QUESTION SCORING (1–5)

9. Are you able to get others to take on activities that affect the organization and positively impact bottom-line results? _____

10. Do you know how to create a committed and excited workforce that is engaged in the projects or activities you are influencing? _____

The following table reflects the meaning of the scores based on my experience. In this book I will be covering some suggested exercises to do in order to improve your skills.

SCORE TOTAL	MEANING
50–46	You are a very good influencer. You are the greatest because you think you are.
45–35	You have got good influence skills and understand what it will take to improve. Go for it!
34–20	You are in the big club of people who think they have good influence skills but don't. You are in need of skill-building help and need to actively work on influence exercises every day.
19–5	Read this book carefully. You can improve, share, and learn to move forward.

2

PRACTICE ACTIVE LISTENING

If you have the skill to speak, you should have the passion to listen.

Alfonso Bucero

Communication is a critical skill for project managers. Some leaders are able to listen but most are always hearing instead of listening. Every time that I think about listening, some images come to my mind regarding the following situation between a project manager and a team member: The team member wants to talk to his project manager because he has a problem or an issue to talk about. The project manager meets him and says, "OK, I'm ready to listen to you. Please tell me about your problem." The team member starts speaking and the project manager does not switch off his cell phone and he continues typing on his personal computer. The team member feels frustrated.

Do you think that project manager is listening to him? My answer is no; this project manager is not present. Are you familiar with this situation? Some project managers do not spend enough time understanding how they communicate to their project team and other project stakeholders. Effective communication among team members is a key for project success. Because of time constraints many people use written communication much more than verbal, but many times we are not aware that body language communication is more than 65%. I learned over the years that not all project managers are conscious of the amount of messages they may transmit to others with their body language, and how those messages may affect them positively or negatively. To communicate well and be a good listener is not easy, but it is not impossible. It takes time, learning from your mistakes, and practice, practice, and practice. In my experience as a project manager, I consider effective communication skills a critical element.

We all need to use a variety of communication techniques to both understand and be understood. If we want to be effective we need to periodically assess our communication skills. Have you thought about what are your communication goals in the project you are managing?

Your goals are probably related changing people's behavior or to get action, ensuring understanding, persuading some team members or stakeholders, or perhaps getting and giving information. In any case you always will have some distortions in communications. There are several factors that affect the sender and the receiver in communication.

For example when we talk about the sender we need to take into account willingness, time, location, cost/consequences, and competition. When we talk about the receiver we need to take into account cost/consequences, role expectations, behavior consistency, sensitivity, timing, appropriateness, belief systems, and motivating factors. What is true is that we need to improve our communication, as 70% of our communication efforts are misunderstood, misinterpreted, rejected, distorted, or not heard. Communication is a critical success factor; the majority of your perceived ability comes from how you communicate.

Practice Active Listening

You, as a project manager, need to work with people and influence them to get successful results. In order to do that you need to develop the ability to listen to people. Not everyone is quick to learn the important lesson of listening. Let me give you an example: Over the years, since I started up my own business, I periodically visited some potential customers with the purpose to sell them my professional services. Because of my passion and beliefs in project management I talked too much in those visits and I listened to them very little. My partner, the sales manager from our organization, who came with me to those visits, advised me to talk less and listen more. However, in many situations I was not conscious about that. I was listening to myself and I was totally blind because of my enthusiasm.

What an idiot I have been! I cannot succeed with others by dumping information on them. If you want to help them or have a positive impact on people, you need to learn how to listen to them. I believe that no one would listen to your talk if he or she didn't know it was his/her turn next. Too many people approach communication that way—they are too busy waiting for their turn to really listen to others.

But people of influence understand the incredible value of becoming a good listener. The ability to skillfully listen is one key to gaining influence with others. Following the advice from Rose, my wife and business partner, I did the following experiment:

1. Pay attention to other people's words when they are speaking instead of trying to answer their questions.
2. Write notes to remember what the other people said.
3. Then prepare your answer. Count from 1 to 5.
4. Answer quietly.

I did that experiment several times and at the beginning it was a complete disaster. I never remembered what the other people said, and I tried to find an answer immediately.

Good listening is effective for several reasons:

- You find out about the person who is talking: what matters to them, what they like and dislike, what they need. They are giving you the information you need to influence them effectively.
- People like talking about themselves, their job, and their challenges. Allow them to do it, be patient with them.
- Listening builds trust and rapport: you appear to be on their side, as opposed to talkers who seem to follow their own agenda.

Good listening is effective, but it is also an art form. You cannot just sit down and hope that a stranger will start discussing his personal life with you. Strangers who do this are often well worth avoiding, especially on public transportation. You need to know how to elicit the right information from the right people. Getting people to talk in a productive and purposeful manner is an art form.

In Figure 2.1 there are five principles to effective listening, which we will explore in detail: open and purposeful questions, reinforcement, paraphrasing, contradiction, and disclosure.

Open and Purposeful Questions

When we first meet someone, it is very tempting to tell them who we are. It is part of our human nature to puff ourselves up a little: we want to make a great impression and show that we are someone who is worth talking to. The problem with this approach is that it is boring.

Figure 2.1   Principles of effective listening.

We may be a source of endless fascination to ourselves, but strangers really do not care. So my suggestion is to ask the person you are meeting to talk about the most interesting subject on the planet. The easiest way to do this is to ask, "What do you do?"

Once they have started talking, keep them talking. Do this by asking open but directed questions. An open question is one where it is impossible to reply yes or no because it encourages a rich answer. Open questions will often start with how, what, or why. For example: What are the major risks of this project? Open-ended types of questions will encourage a rich reply. In opposition, closed questions invite a yes or no answer and may well kill the discussion. For example: Is this activity worthwhile?

Closed questions are dangerous because the answer may not only be short but it may be the wrong answer. Open questions are not random questions.

Let's analyze the following question: What are the major risks/benefits of this project?

You have a choice: ask about the risks first or the benefits first. Your choice of order is likely to determine the success or otherwise of the conversation. If you ask for the risks first, you will get a very rich answer. People are normally risk averse and are very good at spotting risks. You will get a long list of real and imaginary risks. By the time you have heard the answer, there will be little point in asking about the benefits of the idea. The idea will have been crushed under the weight of all the risks and problems that came to light.

If you ask about the benefits first, you may find that you have to push and probe to get all benefits of the new idea fully articulated. But establishing why the idea is a good idea changes the nature of the discussion. If the idea is rich in benefits, then it becomes worthwhile dealing with all the risks that you later identify. Your colleague will have invested personal time and effort in establishing that the idea is good and will be less inclined to drop the idea. By identifying the benefits of the idea, your colleague will have taken ownership of the idea. People rarely oppose their own ideas.

Reinforcement

Go down to your local coffee shop and watch people gossip. You may be able to persuade your boss that this is not just a break from work; it will help your work. First, observe the body language. You will see that people who are deeply engrossed in conversation mirror each other's body shape. When one leans forward, the other leans forward. If one crosses his/her legs, the other will as well. It is like ballet without a choreographer. Everyone does it quite naturally. Now pretend to read a newspaper while you eavesdrop on the conversations. The gossips will be busily supporting and reinforcing each other's worldviews. Right on cue, they will show delight, disgust, shock, surprise, or sympathy with every latest revelation. They will not disbelieve what they are being told, at least not until they recount the story to someone else later. They are making it very easy to talk to each other. They are allies with common interests and common perceptions. The same principles of reinforcement apply to business conversations. If you want someone to talk, make it easy for him/her to talk. Show that you are in tune with them and that you are on their side.

Listening to other people's triumphs and disasters may be boring, but stay focused. Look interested. Make eye contact and stay alert: people quickly pick up lack of interest. Focus 100% of your attention on the person who is talking. When you mind wanders off to planning the next project meeting, worrying about your expense claim and other matters, it shows. When you are focused, people feel flattered and will open up. I said that body language is something that many times we use unconsciously, but a critical part of your communication skills is to better understand body language. Women are better observers than men. And practice is the key. Some of my observations when presenting, talking, or leading a meeting are as follows. Please take them as my observations managing projects. They never are very accurate depending on many environmental circumstances.

My observations are as follows:

1. I'm the boss—Interlacing your hands behind your head, while leaning back in a chair with one leg crossed, sends the signal that you feel comfortable and dominant. Only the senior person in a meeting should do this, as shown in Figure 2.2.
2. I know what I'm talking about—Steepling your fingers means you are confident and focused, as shown in Figure 2.3.

Figure 2.2   I am the boss. (Fotolia image #60503134, ©goodluz/Fotolia.)

Figure 2.3   I know what I'm talking about.

3. I'm confident—Pointing your thumbs skyward means you have a positive outlook. It conveys both confidence and optimism, as shown in Figure 2.4.
4. Hiding your thumbs—Indicates that you are not very sure of yourself. Sticking them in your pockets also makes you look insecure, as shown in Figure 2.5.
5. I'm listening, comfortable, and receptive—A slight head tilt exposes the neck, which people do when they feel they are in a friendly environment. This posture projects a sense of ease, as shown in Figure 2.6.

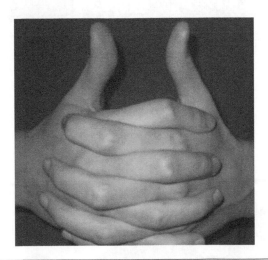

Figure 2.4   I'm confident.

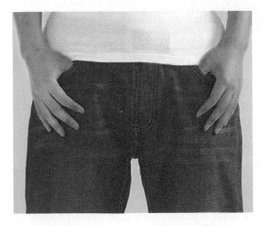

Figure 2.5   Hiding your thumbs.

Figure 2.6   I'm listening and comfortable. (Fotolia image #56977809, ©contrastwerkstatt/ Fotolia.)

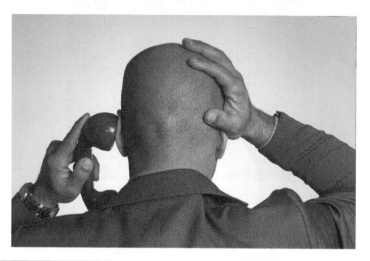

Figure 2.7   I'm uncomfortable. (Fotolia image #47203594, ©gosphotodesign/Fotolia.)

6. I'm uncomfortable and doubtful—Touching the head shows that you are experiencing emotional discomfort or doubt, as shown in Figure 2.7.

7. I'm insecure and concerned—Covering the dimple at the base of your neck means you are fearful or worried, as shown in Figure 2.8.

Now focus on what you say. You don't need to say much. Copy the coffee shop gossips: show that you empathize and agree with the other

Figure 2.8   I'm insecure and concerned. (Fotolia image #5907288, ©Monart Design/Fotolia.)

person. The moment you challenge them, they will close down and stop seeing you as a friend and ally. Reinforcement helps you build the rapport you need when you move on to more substantive discussions.

Paraphrasing

If you want to show your understanding and building agreement, paraphrasing is a useful way. It is simply a summary of what someone has said to you, expressed in your own words. Using paraphrasing you will be able to

1. Show that you have listened properly and that builds empathy with the talker who wants to be heard
2. Be corrected if you have misunderstood
3. Force the listener to listen actively: you will look interested and the talker will respond positively to your apparent interest
4. Be helped remembering key information after the meeting

You need to use paraphrasing with care. You need to be authentic. Use your own words to summarize what has been said. That shows you have really listened and processed what has been said.

You, as a project manager, need to use paraphrasing in a useful way. For example, it is most useful in one-to-one meetings where you want to build rapport. It can also be used in group meetings. By showing you have heard, understood, and respected a colleague, you earn his/ her respect even if you do not agree with each other. You are more likely to have a productive conversation than an argument.

Paraphrasing makes windbags shut up. Have you been in a project meeting where one of the attendees keeps making the same point, in different ways, time and again? Everyone tries to shut him up. The more people try to stop him talking, the more he feels the need to make his point again because he feels he has not been heard. My approach is instead of attacking such people, work with them. Let them have their say concisely and then summarize what was said. Even write it up on a flip chart. You have now amply shown that their point has been made and they have been heard. They can now let the meeting move on.

Contradiction

Contradiction is the other principle of effective listening. Contradiction is not about arguing with people. It is about letting people show off. Let them show how good they are. Let them prove you wrong. Contradiction is a powerful principle to use with professionals who are normally more than keen to showcase their professional talent. The trick is to make the contradiction nonconfrontational: depersonalize it. Because they are the experts, they will win.

When delivering project management workshops I had some experiences with contradiction. For instance, one of the workshop attendees said he did not agree with my point. I answered: "OK, based on your expertise and knowledge what is your opinion about that? Could you give us some details?"

The contradiction may help to clarify some ideas through interaction and discussion. That's great. The goal is contradiction, not conflict. The key to achieving this delicate balance is to depersonalize the contradiction by saying things like: "Other project managers say it is impossible to do this" or "Finance sat this profit forecast is wrong." By doing this, you displace the blame and opprobrium onto other people. You can now work together to prove the rest of the world is wrong. You become allies, not adversaries.

Disclosure

I believe disclosure is a subtle art. It can be badly done. At social events it is common to spot two alpha males fighting like rutting stags. They do it through competitive disclosure. They want to outdo each other's anecdotes: who went on the most exotic holiday, who went to the most prestigious conference, who knows the most important people, and who has the most air miles. Disclosure needs to be slightly more subtle and self-effacing. Tell enough to make the other person want to disclose. Let them "win" by giving you a bigger, better, and more extravagant story than yours. Never threaten or challenge their stories, even if they appear to be 98% fiction.

Active Listening: A Case Study

A colleague with whom I worked in a previous company once demonstrated the power of active listening to me. Mark had been responsible for coordinating the training of a group of senior managers from the European subsidiaries of a large US high-tech company. The training had gone very well and the managing director (MD) of the UK company told Mark he was so convinced that he wanted to use us to carry out work in the UK. The MD made this decision without consulting his three senior divisional sales managers. They were told after the decision had been made and were given a *fait accompli*.

I was appointed as the consultant for the UK group and the day arrived when we had to carry out our first research into the UK client company. I picked up Mark in the morning and as we drove to the client's headquarters he expressed his concern that the divisional sales managers might be somewhat hostile toward us due to the autocratic way in which the project had been decided.

As Mark had all of the connections and knowledge of the client organization, it was agreed that he would take the lead in the three meetings we had scheduled (one with each of the sales managers). I would take a fairly low-key role.

The first meeting was at 10 o'clock. The atmosphere was almost icy. My colleague sat opposite the sales manager who was jacketed and in position behind his large desk. I sat slightly behind and to one side of Mark. It would have been easy for Mark to hide behind the MD's decision and to take the line that it was a *fait accompli* for us all, therefore we had better just get on with it. He did not. He made every effort to really listen to what the first sales manager had to say. He demonstrated this through active listening. He summarized regularly to make sure that he had understood and to demonstrate that he wanted to understand.

From time to time Mark reflected the feelings and concerns of the sales manager, demonstrating that he understood how the sales manager felt about the various subjects we discussed. Expressions such as "So how you see it is ..." and "So your feelings are ..." were a regular feature of the meeting.

After about 30 minutes the atmosphere had significantly changed. Mark and the sales manager were physically closer together. The sales manager drew diagrams and small charts on his pad to explain things that Mark was clearly interested in. Mark had to move into such a position that he could see. The sales manager was by this stage quite comfortable with this. The body language that had started as rather formal and stilted became more expansive and relaxed. At the end of an hour and a half there had clearly been a meeting of minds and one opponent was now open to our involvement, if not yet an advocate.

The second meeting was a rerun of the first. A defensive and totally unconvinced person at the start was converted over the next 90 minutes. We had lunch and Mark and I met with the third of the sales managers. Though not quite as stiff as his other two colleagues, he would have proved a tough nut for most people.

The magic of active listening worked again. In the late afternoon we were on our way back down the motorway with the UK client's most influential people supporting the training that its people were to receive and believing that those who were going to carry it out really understood what was needed and why.

After I drove for a few minutes I turned to Mark and asked him a question. He did not reply. The reason was simple. He was asleep. He was mentally exhausted from the three meetings. For the best part of five hours he had turned up his active listening skills to a very high pitch. That requires motivation, effort, and mental stamina.

Almost everyone who understands what is active listening wants to become good at it. However, few people work on developing it to any level of proficiency. We may be wrong, but we believe that one reason why really good active listening is such a scarce skill is that it does require a lot of mental energy. It is all too easy to nod and say, "Yeah, I understand."

The rarest and finest of skills all take work to master. It is only by application and practice that we will improve. A theoretical understanding of the skill is only the beginning.

Most important, the benefits of active listening will only be fully delivered if we approach the skill as one that is designed to help us help others. If we see active listening as a technique to enable us to manipulate and gain advantage, we should not be surprised if people spot the technique and see us as behaving in an unnatural and false way. Instead of building empathy and trust, the application of the skills as a pure technique will erode the very things we seek to build.

Summary

Listening is not a passive art. It needs skill, focus, and effort to make other people talk constructively, build rapport, and become a trusted partner.

You need to develop the ability to listen to people. No one becomes a good listener overnight; it takes effort and practice.

I would like to share with you some principles of good listening:

- Ask open and purposeful questions
- Reinforce
- Paraphrase
- Contradiction
- Disclosure

Try to practice one at a time. Over the time they will become natural for you. Try to avoid some common mistakes that usually happen:

- Talking over other people

- Asking closed questions
- Indulging in competitive anecdotes

Ask open questions and allow your colleagues, peers, and project stakeholders to give you their opinion. Active listening needs practice. Please be persistent on that.

Try to do the following proposed assessment.

Active Listening Assessment

Score yourself in the following assessment from 0 to 9 (0 is the minimum and 9 is the maximum).

STATEMENT	SCORING (0–9)
1. While listening, I mentally sort out the speaker's ideas in a way that makes sense to me.	_____
2. I stop the speaker and give my opinion when I disagree with something he or she has said.	_____
3. People can often tell when I'm not concentrating on what they are saying.	_____
4. I do not evaluate what a person is saying until he or she has finished talking.	_____
5. When someone takes a long time to present a simple idea, I let my mind wander to other things.	_____
6. I jump into conversations to present my views rather than wait and risk forgetting what I wanted to say.	_____
7. I nod my head and make other gestures to show I am interested in the conversation.	_____
8. I can usually keep focused on what people are saying to me even when they don't sound interesting.	_____
9. Rather than organizing the speaker's ideas, I usually expect the person to summarize them for me.	_____
10. I always say things like "I see" or "uh-huh" so people know that I'm really listening to them.	_____
11. While listening, I concentrate on what is being said and regularly organize the information.	_____
12. While the speaker is talking, I quickly determine whether I like or dislike his/her ideas.	_____
13. I pay close attention to what people are saying even when they are explaining something I already know.	_____
14. I do not give my opinion until I am sure the other person has finished talking.	_____

For your evaluation you need to consider five dimensions:

- Avoiding interruption
- Maintaining interest

- Postponing evaluation
- Organizing information
- Showing interest

These five dimensions represent the total active listening score. Each subdimension has a potential score ranging from 0 to 9 points. The total active listening score has a range from 0 to 45 points.

You need to prepare an action plan based on your observations and the feedback received by your team members, peers, or other project stakeholders.

3

DEVELOP TRUST

Trust is the glue of life. It's the most essential ingredient in effective communication. It's the foundational principle that holds all relationships.

Stephen Covey

Developing trust in the project environment is key for success. Trust is so central to our lives that we take it for granted, like breathing air. We may see ourselves as trustworthy, but that does not count. We have to be seen to be trustworthy by all project stakeholders. Being in a position of authority does not automatically mean that we will be trusted. Some people in authority are trusted, others are not, as can be seen from public attitudes to different professions. Within the workplace, trust is essential. Policy manuals and project management methodologies cannot legislate for trust. The most influential project managers tend to be the most trusted: people are prepared to work with people they trust, not with people they don't trust.

Building trust in relationships with customers, team members, and project stakeholders is an essential skill for all members of a project team. Trust is earned primarily by doing what you say you will do. Follow-through is absolutely critical to building relationships. Trust has to be earned, not claimed. A short example shows how untrustworthy we sound when we claim to be trustworthy. If you heard someone saying this, how much would you trust them?: "Look, Emily, I'm a great project manager, I'm the best.... Of course I'm very honest and I'm not lying, I always manage my team members very well...."

Are you superhero? Probably not. You can hear trust and credibility evaporating like dew in the desert as these words are said. Trust is something every project manager can acquire, with effort. Trust is the function of four elements:

- Sharing common values
- Credibility
- Risk and opportunity
- Distance

Trust is built one person at a time. To build trust we need to know how to manage those elements.

Sharing Common Values

The more we share common values, perceptions, and priorities with someone else, the more we are likely to trust them. If two people share the same pastimes, faith, political outlook, education, or experiences, then they are more likely to trust each other. Most project managers prefer to work with people with whom there is the minimum chance of misunderstanding. The first step in building values alignment is to listen. Listening sympathetically allows the speaker to believe that you respect their worldview. It also allows you to discover what that worldview is. Even if there is much you dislike or disagree with, you should be able to find some areas of common ground.

Focus the conversation on areas of agreement, not disagreement. Even if the only area of agreement is about your favorite films or sports, that is a start in the right direction. Let me share with you the following story: Some months ago a project professional proposed a business collaboration. I had a very small company and he was a free-lancer. Initially I was interested because I have the trend of listening to anybody's proposal. However, as soon as we progressed in our conversations I felt like he valued himself much more than my company and me. I had two more face-to-face meetings with him, but at the end he sent me a draft contract with very uncomfortable clauses for me and my company. His values were different. We were not able to find any common value between us.

Not everybody has the same values. But if we want to be a person of influence we need to, at least, respect other people's values. Showing interest and even admiration for someone else's values is always help-ful to build trust. Respect shows that you are not going to attack or belittle someone for who they are and what they do. And there is always something good to find in anyone. If you can share the same values, or show respect for other people's values, you have made a start in building trust.

Credibility

Every project manager must cultivate not only hard but also soft skills to be successful. Most soft skills are linked to people's attitudes and behaviors. One of the lessons I learned is that organizations need project managers who are honest and competent and can also inspire people. For example: Recently I was involved in a project whose objective was to move one organization from functional to project oriented. I found many resistors from the customer organization and only a few believers. I tried to act honestly with all of them and in many meetings I said, "This change is difficult but not impossible." Today is a good day is my principle. Everything can be changed in the project environment. Also I was very disciplined and always did what I promised. I agreed with my customer to present a project status report every Friday at 10:00 a.m. and I did. If I planned to meet somebody at a determined date, I did. I promised to escalate an issue to top management and I did. I needed to keep on my credibility.

Credibility is built through a set of little details achieved during the project. We must learn from the results and refine our actions. That means credibility. Project management credibility has to do with reputation. Credibility is something that is earned over time. It does not come automatically with the job or the title. It begins early in our lives and careers. A credibility foundation is built step by step during our professional career path. And as each step is achieved, the foundation of the future is gradually built. Credibility can be defined as the behavioral evidence that is used to judge whether a project leader is believable. The most frequent should be they do what they say they will do or they practice what they preach; they walk the talk (Randall L. Englund, "Demonstrating Authenticity and Integrity," *PM Network*).

The credible project manager learns how to discover and communicate the shared values and visions that can form a common ground on which all can stand. Credible leaders find harmony among the diverse interests, points of view, and beliefs. Upon a strong, unified foundation, project leaders and teams can act consistently with spirit and drive to build viable projects.

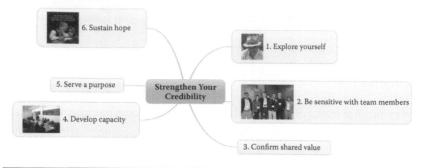

Figure 3.1   Strengthen your credibility.

As a project manager practitioner I suggest some ideas to strengthen your credibility, as shown in Figure 3.1.

1. Exploring yourself—Explore your inner territory. Look into the mirror and ask yourself questions like: Who are you? What do you believe in? What do you stand for? To be credible as a project manager, you must clarify your own values and beliefs. Once clear on your own values, translate them into a set of guiding principles that you communicate to the team you want to lead.

2. Be sensitive with team members—Understand that your own leadership philosophy is only the beginning. To be a leader, you must also develop a deep understanding of the values and desires of your team members. Listen to them. Leadership is a relationship and you will only be able to build that relationship on mutual understanding and respect. Team members come to believe in their leaders, to see them as worthy of their trust, when they believe that the leaders have their best interests at heart.

3. Confirming shared value—Credible leaders honor the diversity of team members. They also find a common ground for agreement on which everyone can stand. They bring people together and join them for a cause. Project leaders show others how everyone's individual values and interests can be served by coming to consensus on a set of common values. Confirm a core of shared values passionately and speak enthusiastically on behalf of the project.

4. Developing capacity—It is essential for project managers to develop continuously the capacity of their members to keep their commitments. Assure that educational opportunities exist for individuals to build their knowledge and skill.

5. Serving a purpose—Leadership is a service. Project leaders serve a purpose for their people who have made it possible for them to lead: their teams.

6. Sustaining hope—Credible leaders keep hope alive. Teams need a positive attitude from their leaders in troubling times of transition. Optimists are proactive and behave in ways that promote health and combat illness. People with high hope are also high achievers.

Project team members expect their leaders to have the courage of their convictions. They expect them to stand up for their beliefs. If leaders are not clear about what they believe in, they are much more likely to change positions with every fad or opinion poll. Without core beliefs and with only shifting positions leaders would be judged as inconsistent and be derided for being political in their behavior.

Managers expect project managers to lead successful projects and achieve good results. Credibility is a condition for project success that must be earned day by day during the project. Walk the talk.

Risk and Opportunity

Risk is the rust in trust. It is corrosive of our ability to trust people. The higher the risk, the less inclined we are to trust strangers. Unless we wish to achieve great poverty, we are unlikely to trust a stranger with our life savings.

Projects are full of risks. Project managers must make decisions every day where the outcome matters but where the conditions surrounding the decision are more or less uncertain. Faced with these circumstances, most project managers have developed habits and strategies to deal with risk for much of the time. It is only in the presence of an unusual risk that people may be conscious of the need to make a choice.

The management of these uncertain situations that matter, also known as risk management, is a discipline in its own right. It has an established role in business, and is applied at a wide range of levels, including management of strategic risk; corporate governance; operational risk; project risk; and health, safety, and the environment. However, risk management is not just important for projects and business. There is increasing interest in the application of effective risk management in society at large, and there is a urgent need for people to embrace appropriate risk taking, both individually and in their working and social groups, supported by government and wider society.

By defining risk simply as uncertainty that matters, it is clear that knowing how to take appropriate risks in any particular situation requires an understanding of two things: the sources and nature of uncertainty, and the degree to which something matters. It is also clear that different things matter to different people to a different extent in different circumstances. As a result, a risk perceived by one person or group as requiring urgent attention may be perceived by others as normal and not worthy of their time.

The perception of risk is not absolute, either present or absent, but is situational and highly dependent on a number of contextual factors. It is this situational aspect of risk that makes the subject of decision making in uncertain situations both fascinating and important.

Taking appropriate risks requires an underlying understanding of the nature of the challenge. On one hand, managing risk can be seen as a rational and logical process requiring a grasp of factual historical evidence combined with mathematical assessments of the likelihood of the uncertain event occurring. It is, however, equally true that managing risk involves the deepest workings of the human brain, as the decisions people make are influenced by a complex interplay of conscious and subconscious factors. This is why one essential component of appropriate risk taking is an understanding of risk attitude as it applies to individuals and to decision-making groups.

Talking about risk leads many people to think only about threats, that is, those uncertainties that should they occur would result in an undesirable outcome. However, contemporary management thinking and practice treats risk in a more balanced way. An uncertain set of circumstances could equally lead to positive outcomes, allowing the definition of risk to encompass both opportunities and threats. This double-sided concept of risk is particularly important in the context of effective decision making, because most decisions need to balance the exploitation or enhancement of hoped-for positive outcomes with the avoidance or mitigation of unwelcome negative ones.

Deciding whether to seize a business opportunity to launch a new product onto the market before the competition needs to be balanced against the threats to the company's reputation if the new product is not trouble free. Although each decision is unique, there are no risk-free options. Moreover, zero risk is not only unachievable, it is also undesirable. Failing to take risk would stifle growth and limit improvement. Appropriate risk-taking promotes competitive advantage and stimulates innovation and creativity. Decision making in a world that is full of "uncertainty that matters" needs to find an optimal balance of threats and opportunities.

The influential project manager will learn to separate rational from emotional responses. Truly logical risks have a pattern all their own:

- They will not be a surprise—The more creative and unexpected the challenge, the more likely it is to be a rational objection hiding an emotional fear.
- They will be presented positively—"How do we deal with ..." rather than "It's impossible because ..."
- They lead to a discussion of solutions.
- They come in small doses rather than vast set of objections.

Logical risks can be dealt with logically. Emotional risks need to be dealt with emotionally.

Distance

The opposite of values of intimacy and credibility is distance. The greater the distance is between two people, the less likely they are to trust each other. I found several types of distance:

- Distance between what we say and what we mean
- Distance between what we say and what is heard
- Distance between your interests and my interests
- Distance between my background, experience, and values and yours

What We Say and What We Mean

The business world uses words to avoid saying it straight. I would like to share with you some of the most difficult words in business:

1. Just—This is used to make a huge request or error seem trivial as in: "Could you just do a complete project report (all lessons learned from a two-years-long project) by Monday?" It is a request best made late on a Friday evening.
2. But—Remember, whatever is said before *but*. "That was a great presentation, but ..." or "I would like to help, but ..."
3. From—Much used by advertisers, as in "Internet broadband connection from $15 per month for six months before the price jumps ..." When you hear *from* be worried for your wallet.
4. Might—It is used to achieve two things: first it sets up a negotiating position as in, "I might be able to do that if ..." Second, it lays the groundwork for excusing failure later on: "I would have done it, if only ..."
5. Only—Closely related to *just*, it is an attempt to make a big request or problem seems small. "It was only a small error..." "We only dropped one nuclear bomb over New York ..."
6. Important (and urgent)—Used to puff up any presentation: "This important new project ..." Important to whom?
7. Strategic—Important, with bells on. Alternately used to justify something that has no financial justification at all.
8. Right size, downsize, best shore, offshore, outsource, optimize—Different forms of saying that there are going to be layoffs.
9. Thank you—This is positive, except for automated voices from call centers.
10. Interesting—Fear this word. "The recession is certainly interesting."
11. Opportunity—In business, all problems have become opportunities.
12. Investment—Spending is bad, but investment is good.

There is some good news in this. The more that jargon and weasel words become endemic, the less managers are trusted. This creates space for managers who used plain words and say what they mean to stand out from the rest of the pack. Sometimes, the art of influence is not too sophisticated. Do the basics right and you will see the difference.

What We Say and What Is Heard

Most of us do not set out to be dishonest. But we can inadvertently set expectations that we cannot meet, as shown in the section on credibility. The problem is not what we say; it is what our colleagues decide to hear. If in doubt, overcommunicate. Based on my experience as a project manager implementing methodologies in organizations, I developed the following rules to cope with that problem. My rationale is as follows:

> First time—Statement not heard amid the noise of other messages.
> Second time—Statement heard but ignored.
> Third time—Statement heard but not really believed.
> Fourth time—Statement heard, believed, and not acted on.
> Fifth time—Something might actually be done.

Besides repetition, consistency and accuracy are essential. Assume that people hear what they want to hear. They will misinterpret what you say to minimize the downside and maximize the upside. If you say something differently five times, they will hear whichever version they want to hear. If you are consistent, there is only one message they can hear.

My Interests and Your Interests

We need to show that we understand, respect, and if necessary adapt to the needs of other people. If all we ever do is to chase our own interests, then few people will feel the need to trust us. Organizations are designed around competing and conflicting interests. Each function and department has a different set of priorities and perspectives.

My Background and Your Background

I find it far easier to deal with project managers, because I think I understand such people. Diversity sounds good in politicians' speeches, but even they do not practice it. The vast majority chooses to live in single-race marriages: daytime diversity leads to sunset segregation.

Even in organizations with a strong conformist culture, different people are … different. Age alone is a great diversifier in everything from personal priorities, experience, and taste in music. Asking a 60-year-old and a 20-year-old to listen to each other's music is normally a recipe for pain and disbelief.

The easiest way to reduce the background gap is to listen actively. Even if you do not share their worldview, by listening you show you respect them. You also learn about them and can find a few areas in common: build on what is common, not on what is different.

Summary

Trust is invisible. Trust needs to be earned, not claimed. It is the invisible force behind the invisible hand of influence. It has to be invisible. The more you openly talk about trust, the less trustworthy you seem. Some people carry the aura of trust around them; others do not. But there is no mystery to this aura. Sharing common values is essential to trust one another. Every project manager needs to develop credibility. Credibility is built through a set of little details achieved during the project. Project team members expect their leaders to have the courage of their convictions. Values, intimacy, and credibility build trust; risk and distance weaken trust. Trust is an absolute vital part of project management. The project management application of trust is something that takes conscious effort to nurture and grow with your professional relationships. Why is it so important? Following are a few reasons.

- People do business with people they trust—You are not going to do business with somebody you do not like or trust. The reverse is true as well. You will do business with someone you like and trust. This principle applies whether it's an internal colleague at your company or a potential client. People must have confidence that you will deliver on your commitments. Recently, I experienced the power of trust in a relationship. I needed to outsource some information technology work for our company. It wasn't a complicated job, but I wanted it to be done right. I knew exactly who to hire, someone I had known for a number of years. I liked their style, knew what they had done for others, and had complete trust in what they would do for me. There was only one catch: Their company policy required up-front payment; undoubtedly a result of having been burned multiple times in the past. It goes against every fiber of my being to pay for work up front, but in this case it didn't seem to matter. I knew the reason for the policy and that they would do the work. It was this high level of trust that enabled them to get my business, and do an outstanding job, by the way. That's the type of project management application of trust you need to apply in your relationships. A high level of trust will allow you to move seemingly unmovable mountains.

- Builds bridges between now and later—How many times have you asked someone to trust you? It may be an individual concerned about his or her future with the company. Or, it may be an entire team uncertain of the future of the project it has been assigned. You may have a vision of the future that they do not. Bridging that gap is another area where the project management application of trust can come into play. You need people to have enough confidence and trust in you that they can bridge the gap between current and future circumstances. Your goal as a project manager is to have your team follow you wherever you go. They may not totally understand the direction you are taking, and may even question it. But they will ultimately follow even if they are not quite sure where you are going.

- Gives you a sense of pride—Having this project management application of trust across your team also gives you a sense of pride. It's a good feeling to look in the mirror and know that you make the right, albeit tough, decisions that are for the greater good of everyone. Actions speak louder than words and your team will pick up on your ability to make trustworthy decisions no matter how big or how small they may be. Trust breeds loyalty within the team and engenders respect for you. Being trusted is one of the most valuable attributes you can have as a project manager, so do not take it for granted.

Trust Assessment

Scoring: The value 1 is the lowest (not true) and 5 is the highest (very true).

STATEMENT	SCORE (1 TO 5)
1. People tell me they're at ease with me. They have a good sense of who I am, they feel they know me, they know what to expect when they see me, talk to me, deal with me.	_____
2. People see me as a logical and clear communicator. What I say makes sense and people compliment me on it.	_____
3. I don't focus on blaming others when things go wrong. I focus on the learning and move on easily from disappointment, without attachment to the past.	_____
4. People tell me I'm honest and open. When I say something, people view it not just as true but as the whole truth. They don't think I'm holding back; they feel I'm giving them the whole picture.	_____
5. I am not afraid to take emotional risks by being open about myself: to acknowledge some failing about myself or to engage in a conversation where I'm not an expert, and to admit my limitations.	_____
6. I am consistent and predictable. People know what to expect from me, and they get it. I am the same person at all times, and the same to all people.	_____
7. In interactions with others, I lead with curiosity. My motivation is less about achieving a goal or preventing loss or embarrassment than it is about asking questions, learning, and discovering ways to improve things for them.	_____
8. People confide in me. They tell me things they often don't tell others; they share with me things they consider private or personal.	_____
9. People can relate to me. They feel at ease and comfortable with me. I fit right in with the way they think and talk and with their interests.	_____
10. My word is my bond. I keep and deliver on my promises. I see keeping my word as a matter of personal integrity.	_____
11. I am not wedded to a particular outcome. I am comfortable changing agendas and objectives, with the end goal of simply making things better for the customer, no matter what result that might entail.	_____
12. I am really good at what I do. I have a lot of expertise in my area, based on experience, talent, and hard work, and people recognize that about me.	_____
13. I am comfortable taking personal risks by engaging with the other person. I know that my intentions are good and am confident that the other person will see that, hence I am comfortable asking questions or raising topics that others in my position might avoid out of fear of appearing controversial or intrusive.	_____
14. I empathize with others and am at ease letting them know it. People have all kinds of feelings; I'm sensitive to them all, and am comfortable sharing my own responses to their feelings, and they know that and appreciate it.	_____

STATEMENT   SCORE (1 TO 5)

15. I'm OK with losing a short-term deal if it improves a long-term
    relationship and helps the other. I believe that behaving that way improves
    the relationship and pays back more strongly over time than being
    opportunistic.   _____

16. I have strong credentials: my degree, my training, my affiliations, and my
    experience are all viewed positively by other people.   _____

17. I work to make sure there are no surprises when I'm around. I use my
    customers' vocabulary; I respect and reflect their norms and environment.
    I make sure that their expectations of me are consistent.   _____

18. I'm known to be discreet. People will talk to me about issues of personal or
    professional concern to them, even if I'm not an expert in that area,
    because they know I'll keep things between us.   _____

19. I do what I say I will do. I am rigorous about follow-through and delivering
    on promises. When I am unable to fulfill a promise, I immediately get in
    communication to reset expectations.   _____

20. I achieve my goals as a by-product of helping customers get theirs. I like
    winning, but I see it as an outcome not a goal, I figure if I help my
    customers win, I will win, too.   _____

SCORE TOTAL   MEANING

100–95   You are a trusted person. You are the greatest because you think you are.

94–65   You have got good trust skills and understand what it will take to improve. Go for
            it!

64–40   You are in the big club of people who think they are trusted but are not. You are in
            need of skill-building help and need to actively work on influence exercises every
            day.

39–19   You need to build up your influence skills. Read and complete all book exercises.
            You can do it. Go for it!

18–1   Read this book carefully. You can improve, share, and learn to move forward.

4

PRACTICE YOUR INTEGRITY

Say what you believe and act on what you say, practicing authenticity and integrity.

Randall L. Englund

Acting on what you say is not always a common practice in our business world. Every time I deliver a project management workshop or seminar I always promise to send the students some examples of the practical exercises we did in the class, and I do it. As my best friend and coauthor Randall L. Englund says, the complete project manager needs to practice authenticity and integrity. Authenticity is to say "what you believe," and integrity is to "act on what you say."

Let me share with you a story: I still remember a senior executive from a multinational company I worked for. He promised the whole project team that he would upgrade their company cars if the project they worked for were successful, but he could not do it because of internal human resource department procedures, so he lost his credibility.

The need for integrity today is perhaps as great as it has ever been. And it is essential for anyone who desires to become a project manager of influence. Integrity is crucial for business and personal success. You can see character issues coming up in every aspect of life. Any project manager who wants to have influence needs to practice integrity (i.e., act on what you say).

In the end you can bend your actions to conform to your principles, or you can bend your principles to conform to your actions. It is a choice you have to make. If you want to become a project manager of influence, then you better choose the path of integrity because all other roads ultimately lead to ruin. To become a project manager of integrity, you need to go back to the fundamentals. You may have to make some tough choices, but they'll be worth it.

Integrity Is Needed to Succeed as a Project Manager

Integrity is very important for your project success, but it is even more critical if you want to be an influencer. It is the foundation upon which many other qualities are built, such as respect, dignity, and trust. If the foundation of integrity is weak, then being a person of influence becomes impossible. Even people who are able to hide their lack of integrity for a period of time eventually experience failure, and whatever influence they temporarily gained disappears. To maintain integrity you need to take care of the little things. Many people misunderstand that. Integrity commits itself to character over personal gain, to people over things, to service over power, to principle over convenience, to the long view over the immediate. Developing and maintaining integrity require constant attention.

I learned some lessons during my professional career that perhaps are three recommendations to act with integrity:

Be impartial—Be fair and objective. Listen to both sides of the story, various opinions, without attaching oneself to any specific one due to prejudice or favoritism. Objective decision making fleshes out the problems and allows teams to get to the bottom of them rather than patching them.

Be thorough—Finish tasks completely, in a comprehensive manner. I find that being thorough in project planning activities means evaluating project requirements and any gaps in details. It also means validating steps against the chosen project management methodology. This ensures a much more comprehensive project management plan and that supporting documentation is produced.

Be focused on the end business result—No matter when team members are introduced, they should verify, within the scope of their project role, initial business requirements and the work that is being requested of them. This allows them to provide their own input based on their subject-matter expertise and strengthens the chances for project success.

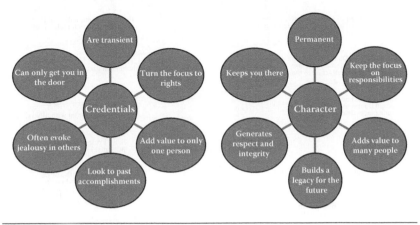

Figure 4.1 Credentials versus character.

Integrity Is an Inside Job

Some project managers struggle with integrity issues because they tend to look outside themselves to explain any deficiencies in character. The development of integrity is an inside job. There are three truths about integrity that go against common thinking:

1. Integrity is not determined by circumstances. It is true that our circumstances affect who we are, especially when we are young. But the older we are, the greater the number of choices we make. Two people can grow up in the same environment, even in the same house, and one has integrity and the other does not. You are responsible for your choices.
2. Integrity is not based on credentials. Character comes from who we are. But some people would like to be judged not by who they are, but by the titles they have earned or the position they hold, regardless of the nature of their character. Look at some differences between the two in Figure 4.1.
3. Integrity is not to be confused with reputation. Some people wrongly emphasize image or reputation. For example: The circumstances amid which you live determine your reputation; the truth you believe determines your character.

How to Measure Your Integrity

I developed some questions that you may use to measure your integrity. Please take your time to answer and reflect on them. After answering

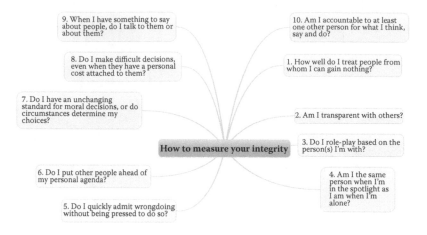

9. When I have something to say about people, do I talk to them or about them?

10. Am I accountable to at least one other person for what I think, say and do?

8. Do I make difficult decisions, even when they have a personal cost attached to them?

1. How well do I treat people from whom I can gain nothing?

7. Do I have an unchanging standard for moral decisions, or do circumstances determine my choices?

2. Am I transparent with others?

How to measure your integrity

3. Do I role-play based on the person(s) I'm with?

6. Do I put other people ahead of my personal agenda?

4. Am I the same person when I'm in the spotlight as I am when I'm alone?

5. Do I quickly admit wrongdoing without being pressed to do so?

Figure 4.2   How to measure your integrity.

those questions, spend some time working on the areas where you had the most trouble. The questions are as follows (see also Figure 4.2).

1. How well do I treat people from whom I can gain nothing? Please reflect upon this question. In many Project Management Institute (PMI) congresses I have seen people approaching the PMI CEO to get some pictures with him, or worse, while I was talking to them about one specific subject and as soon as the CEO went by they left to join the CEO. Are you in that club? Think about it.

2. Am I transparent with others? This question is key for developing your influence. If I am not authentic, what can I expect from somebody else? I met several colleagues who always told me 50% of the real truth. Being honest is not a common behavior I found managing projects in organizations.

3. Do I role-play based on the person(s) I'm with? If you are in the group of people that plays a different role depending on the person(s) they are with, you are not an integrity practitioner. Be yourself, respect yourself and other people will respect you.

4. Am I the same person when I am in the spotlight as I am when I am alone? Being the same person all the time regardless the situation is not easy. But it is possible. You need to practice humility all the time. It is also uncommon, but why not try it?

5. Do I quickly admit wrongdoing without being pressed to do so? It is very difficult for some project managers recognize

their mistakes and errors. Sometimes other people need to remind us. Please be aware of admitting what you did wrong.

6. Do I put other people ahead of my personal agenda? People who belong to professional associations and participate actively answer yes very easily. They are service oriented, and they are frequent givers who practice their generosity. Think about that.

7. Do I have an unchanging standard for moral decisions or do circumstances determine my choices? Reflect on your behavior regarding that. Sometimes circumstances and experiences press you too much.

8. Do I make difficult decisions, even when they have a personal cost attached to them? Project managers, in general, add extra personal time to get things done. What is your behavior on this?

9. When I have something to say about people, do I talk to them or about them? If you want to practice your integrity you need to say to people what you think directly. Being too polite is sometimes an issue.

10. Am I accountable to at least one other person for what I think, say, and do? If you are a project manager, think about your team. What is your behavior?

The path of integrity may not be the easiest one, but it's the only that will get you where you ultimately want to go. Integrity is your best friend. When the people around you know that you are a person of integrity, they know that you want to influence them because of the opportunity to add value to their lives. They don't want to worry about your motives.

Integrity allows others to trust you. And without trust, you have nothing. When you earn people's trust, you begin to earn their confidence, and that is one of the keys to influence. When people begin to trust you, your level of influence increases. And that's when you can start affecting their lives.

Become a Person of Integrity

Let me share with you a personal story: Integrity means honesty, being without blemish, and not lying. We can tell our children this definition and they may or may not listen. What we can be sure of is that they are watching everything you do. I think we would all agree that being honest and living with integrity is an important part of becoming a productive citizen in our community. The question is how do we instill these values in our kids.

We can tell our children a million times what we want them to know and do, and more times than not it will fly right over their heads. They do, however, watch how we live and see when we are not honest or upright. Let's put ourselves in a home atmosphere: You are relaxing, watching your favorite movie, and then the phone rings. You know it is someone wanting you to do them a favor. You tell your child to tell them that you are in the shower. This seems harmless; however, you have just encouraged your child to lie. You have taught them that it is OK as long as no one was harmed by it. Next time get up and go get in the shower! Hold yourself to a higher standard.

Maybe you are at an amusement park buying tickets. Your son just turned thirteen last week, but when the attendant asks you how old your son is, you say twelve. Yes, you just got a cheaper rate; however, do you really think your child does not know how old he is? You just taught him that it is OK to lie as long as you get something good out of it. Hold yourself to a higher standard. Be the example!

I found a teaching aid to use when teaching my children this lesson. I do not remember the source, but it is amazingly effective. I talked with my children about integrity and lying. The group decided that if the lie was little and didn't hurt anyone, it would be OK. We talked about this for some time, adding in that if a movie had just a little bit of bad stuff in it, that was OK, too. You can imagine that we covered many topics and the conclusion was that on all matters "just a little" was OK. I then took out a special pan of brownies and offered it to them explaining that I used a special ingredient in them. I used "just a little" so it should be OK, right?

They insisted that I reveal the ingredient. It was "just a little" DOG POO!

This was a great way to make this point and I will be forever grateful to the source who offered this story! (Whoever it was!)

I am reminded of a song from my childhood and one line stands out to me today: "Oh, be careful little mouth what you say." I repeatedly remind my children so they understand that we are human and make mistakes. However, it is up to us to rectify our errors and hold ourselves accountable for our words and actions. I am not perfect and at times find my integrity lacking. I appreciate the times my children call me on it and give me the opportunity to fix it. It assures me that they understand the importance of this integrity lesson and will begin to apply the principles in their own life. I found some best practices I'd like to share with you regarding how to improve your integrity skills:

1. Commit yourself to honesty, reliability, and confidentiality—Integrity begins with a specific, conscious decision. If you wait until a moment of crisis before settling your integrity issues, you set yourself up to fail. Choose today to live by strict moral code and determine to stick with it no matter what happens. Be honest with all your project stakeholders and act on what you say during the whole project life cycle at every project you manage. Practice and respect the PMI code of ethics as a professional project manager.

2. Decide ahead of time that you don't have a price—I really believe that few men have the virtue to withstand the highest bidder. Some people can be bought because they haven't settled the money issue before the moment of temptation. One of the ways to guard yourself against a breach in integrity is to make a decision today that you won't sell your integrity: not for power, revenge, pride, or money. For instance, when I was a PMI chapter president I was tempted by unprofessional people to accept some presents to make decisions in their favor. That unacceptable behavior exists in almost all countries where those practices are allowed and accepted.

3. Major in the minor things—The little things make or break us. If you cross the line of your values, whether it is by an inch or by a mile, you are still out of bounds. Honesty is a habit you ingrain by doing the right thing all the time, day after day, week after week, year after year. If you consistently do what's right in the little things, you're less likely to wander off course morally or ethically. Take care of the details with your team members every day.

4. Each day, do what you should do before what you want to do—A big part of integrity is following through consistently on your responsibilities. When you do the things you have to do when you have to do them, the day will come when you can do the things you want to do when you want to do them. Everybody ought to do some least favorite things everyday just for the practice. When you practice integrity you earn freedom. When you have freedom you inspire people. Indirectly you will influence people when you practice integrity in managing projects in organizations. Today is a good day to start, so please start.

Importance of Integrity

One of the things that I value most is integrity. I don't mean in the ethical sense but more toward truth and reliability. You might think of it along the lines of "I am my word." Why? Because of time. It is probably our most valuable resource. Yes, your health and your mind matter quite substantially, too, but at least with time you can work on both of these. Without time, you don't have the power to change anything.

So, as you might imagine, I highly value my time. Minutes, hours, days wasted could have been spent doing more productive, rewarding, or exciting things. As a result, when I say "I'll be there at 7 p.m.," I mean it. This is because I believe that another person's time is no more or less valuable than my own. I do not believe that I have a right to waste one of their most precious resources by making them wait. When I say "I'll get that done," I mean it. This is because I have created the expectation that something will happen, from which another might make plans. If I don't follow through on my promise, then I will probably have ended up wasting another person's time.

I do these things, partly to lead by example, partly because I believe it's just plain, decent respect, and partly because when I repeatedly deliver on my promises, I gain another's trust in me. On the other hand, if you can't commit to something, then why not say that up front? I believe that's better than creating the expectation that you will live up to your word and then failing to do so.

Project Management Integrity

Integrity is one of those old-fashioned words. It gets thrown in with words like horseless carriage, nifty and swell, house calls, and milkman. It has been replaced by ideas like politics, expedience, and sales calls. One sales guy I worked with summed up integrity in the workplace by saying, "Pick us 'cause we aren't as slimy as the competition."

Maintaining your integrity is a full-time job, but it can make all the difference in affecting your reputation. Here are a few reminders to help you out. As a project manager, *integrity* may be defined as consistency of actions, values, methods, measures, principles, expectations, and outcome. As a holistic concept, it judges the quality of a system in terms of its ability to achieve its own goals.

"Integrity is doing the right thing, especially when no one is watching."

"Integrity is doing what you say you'll do, and saying what you truly think, even if unpopular."

Be on time—Do you show up to meetings when you get around to it, arriving five to ten minutes late? Or dial into conference calls late? Are your meetings back to back? Why not start your meetings 10 to 15 minutes past the hour to give people time to walk from one meeting to the next? Kind of like high school, remember? I was taught that if you are not early, you're late—and that is so true!

Do what you said you will do—Is your yes really a yes? I know people who say yes but have no intentions of doing it. That is not being accountable. When you commit to a deadline, meet it. If you anticipate a problem, then tell the PM and he or she can help mitigate things. Or else you are late, making others late, and so on! It is a vicious cycle.

Take responsibility—As the PM, you own the success of the project. I once heard a statement at a PMI seminar: "If it is to be, it's up to me" and that is as true as you can get. That doesn't mean doing everything, but it does mean you need to remember that if a project team member fails or stumbles that you are there to help him or her succeed, mitigate the issue, come up with plan B, C, and so on. You are responsible for the project's success.

Put in an honest day's work—Do you work 40 hours a week, or do you come in late and leave early? Do you surf the web at work or talk on phone or text, tweet, or blog? Your employer pays you to be productive. I hate to be bored with slow work, so find a need and fill it, or ask for something more to do.

Report accurately—Be honest with your time sheet, status report, budget, schedule, milestones, risks, and so on. State it positively to keep your team and management informed. Nothing is worse than surprises when you knew it might happen. Think about it. Would you hire you knowing what you do?

Summary

If you know what you stand for and act accordingly, people can trust you. You are a model of the character and consistency that other people admire and want to emulate. And you have laid a good foundation, one that makes it possible for you to become a person of positive influence in their lives. But sometimes people make things wrong, they are late or overcommitted, they are not perfect. In that case my advice is to reflect upon your behavior and please think if you believe that is the way of influencing positively your team members and other project stakeholders. Do not promise anybody something that you are not sure to achieve. Ask yourself if you are acting on what you said. If you want to become a project manager of influence, then you better choose the path of integrity because all other roads ultimately lead to ruin. To become a project manager of integrity, you need to go back to the fundamentals. You may have to make some tough choices, but they'll be worth it.

To maintain integrity you need to take care of the little things. Integrity allows others to trust you. And without trust, you have nothing. When you earn people's trust, you begin to earn their confidence, and that is one of the keys to influence. Every project manager is a leader in your organization, whether the teams they lead have five people or fifty people on them. Your project managers are representing your organization, as well as the project, to your clients. So I think it's useful to ask what integrity means in the project management world.

Here are some of the behaviors I look for when I am seeking integrity:

1. A PM who tells the truth using simple language, without distorting facts or manipulating people.

2. A PM who doesn't try to hide information; in fact, he or she sets up tools and reports that enable him or her to create project transparency (e.g., status, schedule, running rate) without being forced to do so.

3. A PM who keeps his or her commitments and delivers the results promised; a PM with a track record for delivering results over a number of projects.

4. A PM who is accountable for the project status and results, who takes responsibility for the end results without pointing fingers at others. A PM who has this trait is also likely to hold his or her individual team members accountable for results.

5. A PM who confronts tough issues directly and can discuss the issues honestly, even when people don't like the answer.

Influence Checklist

Commit yourself to developing strong character as a project manager:

- In the past, have you made it a practice to take full responsibility for your character? It's something that you need to do in order to become a person of influence.
- Set aside the negative experiences you have had, including difficult circumstances and people who have hurt you.
- Forget about your credentials as a project manager or the reputation you have built over the years.
- Strip all that away, and look at what's left.
- If you don't see solid integrity in yourself, make the commitment to change today.
- Do the little things. Spend the next week carefully monitoring your character habits. Make a note to yourself each time you do any of the following:
  - Do not tell the whole truth
  - Neglect to fulfill a commitment, whether it is promised or implied
  - Leave an assignment uncompleted
  - Talk about something that you might have been expected to keep in confidence

HAVING INTEGRITY WITH YOUR TEAM MEMBERS AND OTHER PROJECT STAKEHOLDERS

- *Read the following statement, and then sign the line below:*

  I commit myself to being a project manager who practices integrity. Truth, reliability, honesty, and confidentiality will be the foundation of my professional life. I will treat others as I expect to be treated. I will live according to the highest standards of integrity facing up to all projects' circumstances.

  Signature: _____ Date: _____

- Do what you should do before you do what you want to do. Every day this week, find two items on your to-do list that you should do but that you have been putting off.
- Complete those tasks before doing anything on the list that you enjoy.

5

INFLUENCE TO WIN

If you don't see yourself as a winner, then you cannot perform as a winner.

Zig Ziglar

Project managers are always in competition for the limited management time, budget, bonuses, and promotions when managing projects in organizations. The real competition is not on the customer site; it is sitting at the desk near you. The result is a world of win–lose. Let me share with you the following story.

I can still remember when working for a multinational organization competing for an assignment as a project manager for a savings bank customer. I was competing with another colleague younger than me. He had no family constraints, and he was single. There was a customer project to be managed far away from Madrid, the city of my residence. My young competitor was a successful project manager, but he only had five years of experience managing similar projects. Being single he had no family restrictions in his temporary move to a new city. I had twenty years of experience, but I was married with family constraints. From my organization perspective, I was paid a higher salary than my colleague, so my labor cost was higher for my company; however, I had much more experience. My manager was worried about delivering maximum value to our customer, but he was worried about my cost and its impact in the customer project budget. He needed to make a decision. Then, I proposed to my manager the following solution:

1. Assigning me as a project manager, based on my experience and performance, for at least the first six months of the project

2. Assigning my young colleague as a backup project manager who would spend only half the time with me in order to be better prepared for the future on that project

3. Assigning my young colleague six months later as a project manager

I explained to my manager that approach would be more effective for the organization, first; for our customer, who would see his project reinforced in terms of project management; and also for my colleague. This was a real example of influencing to win. My manager spent some time to make his decision, but when he made it he appreciated the benefits and the customer felt happy.

Achieving a Win–Win Discussion

There are four main strands of achieving a win–win discussion, as shown at Figure 5.1: (1) focus on interests, (2) offer options, (3) craft a story, and (4) agree in public, argue in private.

Focus on Interests

The most vicious arguments are win–lose arguments. What is at stake is not just the rational outcome about who gets the better part of the deal. There is also a huge amount of emotional capital at stake: Who is seen to have won? The best way to win any war is without fighting. Instead of using the force, use creativity to change the rules of engagement.

Telling people to get creative is not helpful. And creativity workshops do not help either; they give creativity a bad name. Being asked

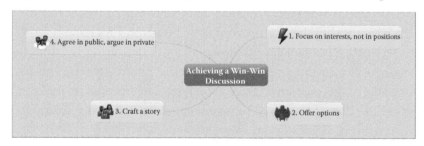

Figure 5.1   The steps for achieving a win–win discussion.

Table 5.1 Interests behind the Position

POSITION	COUNTERPOSITION
I need a 30% pay raise.	Company policy allows a 10% raise.
Give me a 25% discount on this purchase.	No, I can't take a loss.
Cut your budget 15% for next year.	There is nothing left to cut.
I want to be promoted.	No promotions are available.

what sort of flower you would be if you were a flower is bad enough. Behaving like that flower is worse. Fortunately, there is method to being creative when it comes to influential discussions. The principle is simple: Find the interests behind the position (see Table 5.1).

The challenge is to understand the interest that lies behind the position. To start, look at the following example of the classic pay and promotion discussion.

Turning a Pay Promotion Discussion into a Win–Win–Win

Rose is a project manager from Spain. She had done extremely well in her first two years as a project manager. She felt she was now due a pay raise and a promotion. Her manager, Beatriz, had little budget and not much flexibility on promotions. Rose and her manager had completely opposite positions: pay raise and promotion versus no raise and no promotion. War started. How could they avoid a win–lose battle over their respective positions?

Fortunately, they both had a passionate commitment to improve project management in Spain. They had a common interest at a very high level, but there was still a huge gap to convert that interest into a practical way forward. Being a project manager, Rose did her homework before meeting her manager. She figured out they had three more common interests:

- She wanted to stay. Her manager needed her to stay. Attracting quality staff was time-consuming, expensive, and fraught with risk.
- She wanted more responsibility. Her manager had several ideas about a project management soft skills training program and she needed an instructor for that.

- She wanted to build her career and get a master's degree. The manager was under pressure to show the top management what she was doing about professional development.

When they met, Beatriz was mightily relieved to find that Rose did not ask for the expected pay raise and promotion. It was a much more useful discussion about what she would do if she stayed. Eventually, they agreed that she would lead the soft skills training area across the company, which would give her credits toward the master's degree she was working on.

Finally, Rose asked Beatriz how she could help on pay and position. Too late, Beatriz realized she had been put on the spot. She had to do something for Rose. There was a long pause. She realized that with Rose leading the soft skills training area would save costs versus bringing in outside help.

Retaining Rose would also save on the costs and risks of recruiting a replacement. Rose was helping Beatriz save some precious budget; Beatriz could afford to share some of the savings with Rose. In the end Rose got less than she had asked for, but more than she had expected. More important, both Rose and Beatriz left feeling that they had achieved a very satisfactory outcome. Neither had achieved their original position, but they had fulfilled their common interests.

Once you find the interest behind the position, you have a chance of exploring more options. You no longer have a win–lose discussion. The potential for a win–win–win starts to emerge. People rarely volunteer these positions. Quite often they do not even know what their real interests are: they have become so fixated on winning a battle over price or something else that they have ignored the wider picture. You have to help them discover their real interests.

Once you do this you not only change the nature of the discussion, but you also change the nature of the relationship. You are no longer their adversary, you are their adviser. That is a far better position to be in.

There are two simple ways you can discover someone's real interests:

1. Do your homework. Most positions are in some way predictable. And equally, the interests behind the position are also
   fairly predictable. If you have properly prepared, you are in a
   better position to use the next two discovery methods.
2. Offer some alternatives. Once you have done your homework, you should know what the typical alternatives are to
   the positions you are in. We will explore this further in the
   next section.

Win–lose discussions are natural but unproductive. Influencers
learn that winning allies is more important than winning arguments
in the long term. When it comes to the next discussion, the loser in a
win–lose discussion will be out for revenge. In contrast, the influencers have much easier rides to a win–win with their allies. Focusing
on common interests rather than individual positions is the first step
toward achieving a win–win.

Offer Options

Be creative offering options to the other party. Use your creativity
maintaining the win–win attitude in your mind, and facilitating the
other part to reflect about a set of new possibilities to help each other.
There is nothing to bargain over except who gets the largest slice of
the cake. But once you have got behind the stated position to someone's interests, you find a range of options open up.

The normal challenge in this discussion is that the person you are
talking with has simply not thought of all the options. They have
come in prepared for a negotiation that they want to win. Having
put their boxing gloves on, they want to have the bout. To get to
the options discussion, you have to deploy other key strategies of the
effective influencer:

1. Listen. Let them talk about their needs and wants.
2. Ask smart questions. Do not make smart statements and do
   not challenge them. If you do that, then they will put their
   boxing gloves back on and the bout will start.

Project Management Training Course Value: Price versus Package

My colleague Tom visited a project management services provider office to register for a project management training course. The sales manager and he did not have much of a common interest. The sales manager wanted to make as much money, and Tom wanted to spend as little money as possible for his training course registration, although he was looking for a good-quality training course. Tom figured he had $1,000 to spend on his course registration. It looked like they were going to have a head-on collision over price.

But the sales manager was smart. First, he took time to listen to what Tom wanted. Good start. Then the sales manager suggested a registration course that was within Tom's budget. The instructor for that course had only five years of experience, but the sales manager told Tom that his level of knowledge was high and the level of quality would be enough for him. This showed Tom could trust him. He was not trying to escalate Tom into a higher price. And then Tom got confused, which was really smart.

First, there is a choice of training courses around instructor experience, more exercises, and ten hours of mentoring service for the course attendee after the training. The choice was bewildering. Tom realized that focus on price was too simple: Tom needed to think harder about cost and value.

By the time Tom had worked all the choices, his head was reeling. Fortunately, the sales manager made it easy for him. He reduced the choice to just two packages that seemed to suit Tom best: one at $250 a month for four months, the other at $500 a month for two months. To make it easy for Tom, the sales manager threw in some extra service: eight hours of coaching after the training. He had offered Tom a concession, an apparent win. It was a concession that was standard practice, but it gave Tom the sense he was winning. Tom bought the training course and was happy to have got a bargain, which cost him more than he had originally budgeted.

By offering choices, the manager got away from the simple price discussion; it was now a price–value discussion. A price discussion is win–lose. Price–value can be a win–win discussion.

Craft a Story

Humans are risk averse. Risk aversion saved our ancestors from becoming breakfast for a saber tooth tiger. When we talk about risk, we normally think of rational risk, for example: Will this product be defective?

But the much bigger risk is personal and emotional: Will I look stupid if I make this decision? Even photocopiers are an emotional purchase. What on earth can be emotional about a photocopier? It should be a rational decision about copy speed, quality, reliability, overall cost, and cost per sheet. Simple. Except it is not that simple. If you are buying the photocopier for the office and it keeps breaking, you become the office idiot. Every time there is an urgent copy job that goes wrong, you get the blame. You are not just the office idiot; you are the office object of hate. Suddenly, all the discussion about saving 0.1 cents per sheet of paper looks irrelevant.

As an exercise, think about the last time you managed a project. Will you tell your friends and colleagues that you got a lousy project? Or will you tell a story that shows you got a pretty good project and you are a smart project manager. Most humans like to show that they are smart. So what is the story that you will craft? There are plenty of ways you can show you got a good project:

- Great opportunity to add value to my customer
- Good lessons learned to do more projects with my customer
- Good project-sponsor involvement
- Good support from my customer
- Great results and good profit

It is a story you probably use with friends and colleagues if ever asked about the project you got. The art of crafting a story is to give the other person a win. Let them have something to brag about. The more options you can create, the more you can find a way of letting them win something.

Many of the options that a mobile phone seller or car salesperson offer have low cost to them but high value to the buyer; they are easy wins to give. But the smart influencer does not make them appear easy. They give the concessions with the appearance of great regret: "This is not normal at all. I will have to ask my manager" or "I've never done this before, but in your case ..." The more reluctant you appear, the more the other side is convinced that they have won a great prize. You are quietly flattering their ego. You are giving them a story whose message they value: "I am a smart sort of person."

Agree in Public, Argue in Private

You need to make public agreements to advance in a win–win discussion. Summarizing achievements is quite essential to progress in any discussion. People need to feel they are advancing and obtaining some kind of mutual benefits from two parts.

As soon as someone says something in public, they are committed. They cannot unwind their position without loss of face. Notice how politicians go through yoga-like contortions to avoid changing a public position, even when any sane view of their situation would demand a change. In the workplace, as soon as someone says that won't work, they are committed; they will find more or less any reason to justify their initial instinct.

For the purposes of influencing, the critical distinction is between public and private. Any meeting where there are more than two people present is public. Introducing a third person means the discussion is no longer in confidence.

For this reason, most influencing happens quietly behind closed doors and on a one-on-one basis. The purpose of a meeting, for an influencer, is never to make a decision. The value of a public meeting (with more than two people present) is to give public confirmation to all the deals that have been struck in private. Each person around the table wants the comfort of knowing that they are not alone in supporting your brilliant or crazy idea. Collective agreement is important. If everyone agrees, then no one can be singled out if things go wrong later on.

If there is one person who cannot be influenced in private, then at least the private discussion allows you to do three things that help:

1. You understand why the person disagrees. You cannot narrow the disagreement to one or two highly specific issues.
2. You build a coalition of support, which isolates the person who disagrees. Once he or she sees the power of the coalition

he or she will normally back down, having made his or her various points.

3. You have followed fair process. You have given the individual a chance to be heard. This show of respect draws much of the sting and venom out of the opposition.

Keep doubts and opposition private; make agreements public.

The Winners

According to Rosabeth Moss Kanter ("How Leaders Gain and Lose Confidence," *Leader to Leader*, no. 35 winter 2005, 21–27) forward-thinking leaders create a foundation for confidence that permits people to achieve high levels of performance, and do it as part of a successful team. She says every time you win, your confidence is increased. Winning begets winning, because it produces confidence at four levels:

- Self-confidence—The result of an emotional climate of aiming high and expecting to reach the target. Feeling good.
- Confidence in one another—This is fostered by positive, supportive, team-oriented behavior that makes people more engaged with their tasks and with one another.
- Confidence in the system—This makes it possible to transmit problem-solving and team-enhancing behavior to new people and keep the winning streak going.
- External confidence—Driven by a network to provide resources that attract media attention, financial backers, and opinion leader support.

Winning streaks are characterized by truth telling, continuity, and continued investment. Success is neither magic nor dumb luck; it stems from a great deal of consistent hard work to perfect each detail—it is even a little mundane.

Why Do Winning Streaks End?

If winners accumulate so many advantages, why do cycles of success ever end? Winning means continuous efforts are never easy. Project managers find a lot of difficulties on winning with project stakeholders when managing projects, but they must not give up when they run into difficulties. That way they will influence them positively to continue winning.

Several factors are involved in winning. Confidence fuels winning but arrogance can destroy it. When the project manager is a good motivator and he or she recognizes the efforts and the work well done, people gain confidence. Arrogance cover-ups and enemy blaming makes people lose sight of reality as they fly high in their fantasies, and when they are no longer grounded, they are tempted to panic at the first signs of trouble.

When winners keep their heads under pressure, they are better equipped to recover from fumbles. But when they become complacent, take winning for granted, begin to believe with little evidence that they can succeed in untested realms, and neglect to mine the foundations supporting them, then winners begin to lose.

I have managed many projects in my career in different countries and in order to develop a winning team, try the following influence strategies:

1. Look at the future—Many companies avoid team building because of past experiences that have left employees jaded and cynical. This situation often results from one too many faddish "innovations" in management. Change never comes magically. Any significant change in your organization requires a fundamental shift in the way you think, act, and do business. To succeed, you have to start thinking in terms of your real customers and what they want. If you are a manager or owner, then your real customers are your employees. You must think of their needs first, and let them think of the needs of the external customers.

2. Become a leader—You must use your strengths (whatever they are) to bring out the best in others. You need to focus only on your strengths and stop focusing on weaknesses. Your people need you to be their leader. Think about what your strengths are and how to use them to bring out the best in others. Ask your people what they think your strengths are. You will get remarkably different answers than the ones you listed. Then get about using your strengths to build your winning team, and let it bring out the best in your customers.

3. Inspire people
   - Commitment—It is necessary that you live the mission and expect the whole team to follow your example.
   - Cooperation—The whole must become greater than the sum of the parts.
   - Communication—Provide all necessary information, and let the team members know that it is OK to ask for information and to share data with each other, fellow workers, and sometimes even customers.
   - Contribution—Participation is not optional in a teamwork situation. You must require and support it.
4. Encourage your team—People do exactly what you reward them for doing. They do not respond to promises, requests, cries, screams, threats, or kindness. They respond to action. Reward the individual members and the team for the results you really want, and only for the results you really want.
5. Be a difference maker—Every member and the team as a whole need to feel that they are making a difference in the lives of others. The efforts they make are not just about business success; they are about pride, about having their work mean something to someone. You must discover what that meaning is and magnify it. Let them clearly see the value of what they are doing and why it matters. Let them feel the pride in their success.
6. Communicate the results—Teams need to feel a sense of accomplishment; they need to see the end result of a project. Assign your team whole projects, not pieces. Assign results, not specific tasks. Let team members carry the project from start to finish. And make sure others know about the finished product and its importance. That will help team members feel the accomplishment of completing something significant.
7. Allow your people time for training—You must provide training for the team members and the leaders because it is a necessary ingredient for team success. Allow training on any topic that the team wants (regardless of whether it is job related) using videotapes, audiotapes, seminars, books, and professional trainers. Studies show a return of ten to thirty times the initial financial investment in training, and it does

not matter what a team or its individual members learn. So keep everyone engaged in learning. Any voluntary expansion of their abilities is a good thing for your organization.

8. Offer them a challenge—Everyone has limits. But how will your team members ever know what their limits are if you never give them a project that is more difficult than they thought they could accomplish? They need to learn and grow, to develop and improve. They need you to challenge them and to believe in them. Once you issue the challenge, you must confidently assure them that you have faith in them. But always keep an open door and encourage the team to come to you when they feel ill equipped to handle a problem.

9. Empower the team—Give full control to the team: responsibility, authority, and accountability. This means full delegation. Don't look over members' shoulders, don't question their expenses, and don't ask them to explain every decision and every action. When you give them a project, you also need to outline their boundaries (e.g., budget, timetable, scope of responsibility, and authority). Then let them carry the ball. Meet with them at agreed-upon times and keep your door open in case they need to call on you. Other than that, get out of the way and let them impress you.

10. Be respectful—When they rise to the challenge and accomplish something truly outstanding, you must show your appreciation for their efforts, and reward the team accordingly. Let them see the respect you have for their significant accomplishments, and make certain others see it as well. The sweetest sound in the world is one's own name being spoken in a complimentary fashion by someone else. Let them hear their names and the name of the team from your lips to every ear in the organization.

Persistence

Ever been on a roll with your business when you felt invincible? No matter what you touched, it turned to gold? And then all of a sudden, out of nowhere, a zinger comes your way that totally disrupts your life and your business? Past performance shifts expectations. Losing streaks create pressure and are characterized by disruption and lack of investment. They tempt people to behave in ways that erode their ability to solve problems and cause them to lose confidence in themselves, in one another, and in their leaders. When losses continue, often as a direct result of blame, turf protection, or passivity, something larger occurs. Once the "loser" label is slapped on, those suffering losses are set up to fail. They find it harder to get support and opportunity. They are targeted, pressured, distracted, punished, second-guessed, shunned, marginalized, ruled against, starved, or tempted to cut corners. Despair can cause acts of desperation.

How to Break Out and Master a Turnaround

In order to deal with or stop a losing streak, I face the reality and try to inspire confidence in my people through cooperation and collaboration. You are a leader; you need to be a believer but also preach by example. The only way to get a winning streak back is to practice discipline and embrace responsibility at the highest level of excellence. Inspire your people through creating commitment. That builds self-confidence, confidence in others, and confidence that the whole system can deliver on its promises. Your behaviors in those moments will make the difference, you can influence them to win, and they are your followers.

Summary

- Winning is about creativity. It depends on seeing the world through the eyes of the person you wish to influence. You cannot offer them a win unless you know what a win looks like for them. And the good news is that the win for them is about perception as much as reality. Find a concession, an offer that makes them look good in their own eyes and in the eyes of their peers.
- To find a win–win requires creativity. Creativity can come from innate genius on the spur of the moment and some of it can come from experience. A more reliable way of being creative is to work as a team. Prepare sales calls, negotiations, and important meetings with the help of your team. The more

you discuss it, the more options, potential concessions, and wins–wins appear. You gain more insight into how the other party thinks. Spontaneity is best when it is well rehearsed.

- The win–lose mind-set can win today's battle. But it makes it much harder to win tomorrow's battle: the loser will be twice as resistant next time around. The win–win allows you to win without fighting today. It then makes it even easier to win again next time, because you have an ally rather than an enemy.

- Please go to the next section and try to answer the listed questions to assess your abilities and skills as a winner.

Winning Checklist

STATEMENT	ANSWER (YES OR NO)
1. The only way to get the best of an argument is to avoid it.	_____
2. Show respect for the other person's opinions. Never say "you're wrong."	_____
3. If you're wrong, admit it quickly and emphatically.	_____
4. Begin in a friendly way.	_____
5. Start with questions to which the other person will answer yes.	_____
6. Let the other person do a great deal of the talking.	_____
7. Let the other person feel the idea is his or hers.	_____
8. Try honestly to see things from the other person's point of view.	_____
9. Be sympathetic with the other person's ideas and desires.	_____
10. Appeal to the nobler motives.	_____
11. Dramatize your ideas.	_____
12. Throw down a challenge.	_____

Scoring guidelines: You need to answer yes or no to each question in order to help you plan for improvement on your winning skills as a project manager.

6

PRACTICE YOUR GENEROSITY

> Let us try to teach generosity and altruism, because we are born selfish.

> **Richard Dawkins**

Generosity is one of the core qualities people look for in their leaders. And it's not just generosity with money. In fact, research shows other things are more important to people, in terms of what they hoped for from their leaders. People want leaders to be generous with knowledge, time, credit, power, information, and faith. It is really hard to trust and fully support a leader who is stingy, who seems to be in competition with you, or who does not believe in your potential. The influencer needs to develop a network of alliances, mutual obligations, and debts, and that way he or she will invest in the future. Influence is a reciprocal relationship.

By generosity we mean the quality of being kind, understanding, and not selfish; the quality of being generous, especially the willingness to give valuable things to others. Project manager generosity is a scarce commodity. As projects grow harder and meaner, generosity becomes even scarcer. As generosity becomes scarcer, it becomes more valuable. As a project manager needs to influence, it takes a long-term perspective: generosity is all about self-interest in the long term. It helps a lot to build willing partners, supporters, and allies in your projects. The hand in the Figure 6.1 shows the action of a giver.

You, as a project manager, should use influential generosity that I would like to distinguish by four characteristics: customized, earned, measured, and requested. I believe that these characteristics count because they maximize the chances of the generosity being valued and reciprocated. When we follow the right principles, we can acquire allies and supporters who will help us when we need help.

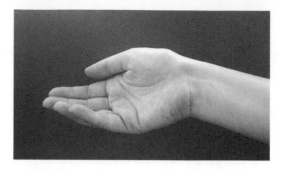

Figure 6.1   Generosity.

Let me give you an example that will show how to be generous effectively:

When working at a multinational company as a project manager, a senior manager wanted me to move into his department. I did not know him very well, although he appeared to be supervising and sponsoring some interesting projects. I was managing a critical project in my department and was not very interested in listening to his overtures. The truth was that I had a lack of time to do other tasks. Eventually, he persuaded me to deliver a small presentation to his team on my current project. It was a chance to show off; it was easy to do and I was allowed to pick the time and place for the presentation (easy give). And I was being set up without knowing it.

At my presentation everybody was very kind and flattering. A few days later, a box with a high-quality bottle of wine arrived on my desk: the senior manager had done his homework and had even found out which wine brand I liked most. I rarely bought it because it was very expensive.

This story covers three of the four characteristics of generosity:

1. It was highly *customized* to my interests and needs. It showed that he cared. My existing boss had no clue what I liked or did not like, and did not seem to care.
2. The gift felt like it had been *earned*, and so I valued it. It was not just a gift; it was recognition of work well done, and recognition is always welcome.

3. It was a *measured* gift. He did not shower me with presents. That would have been bribery. I could not get something for nothing; rewards need to be earned.

This manager then asked me for another favor, helping him on an existing project (the fourth characteristic of generosity: requesting help). I helped and was given more recognition. He had set up the process of give and take. We were creating some mutual obligations. Incrementally, I was being committed to him and split from my existing boss. After a couple of months I willingly made the switch.

By "giving to take," I mean you need to give something to somebody if you want to have the possibility to take something. In my opinion it is a powerful way of building commitment. Let's see how the four principles of giving to take can be applied in practice. In fact I usually apply this approach when managing my project team members and other project stakeholders.

Customized Generosity

Generosity is not just about gifts. These things have monetary value but not necessarily personal value. The most precious resources in an organization tend to be things like time and recognition. When you give people your time, you are investing your most precious and limited resource in them and people respond to that vote of confidence. Let me give you an example: Last year, after a PMI Congress, a colleague from Nigeria approached and asked me if I wanted to be his mentor. I immediately said yes. We had been in touch for one year and the result had been great. He learned from me and I learned from him. We had developed a good relationship. We did it virtually; we are physically far away but we exchange e-mails, chats, and so on. I did not expect anything in exchange. He gave me the great opportunity to give and share, and there is no money to pay that.

I strongly recommend that you mentor somebody. Develop your generosity, be a giver and you will take many great intangible things that gratify and satisfy you, first, as a person and, second, as a professional. Step by step you will develop a network of alliances and mutual debts. The influencer needs to invest in the future.

When you give people recognition, it is also a vote of confidence in them. Once you have made the investment, you can expect to ask for a return on that investment and most people will give willingly. That way you have set up the process of give and take.

Earned Generosity

As a general rule, we value what we earn more than what is free. For example, when I worked for Hewlett-Packard in Spain, I found salespeople would compete to win the monthly prize, which would often be considered a token, perhaps a nice pen or a dinner out. At the annual kickoff meeting the salespeople would be inundated with free pens and meals, and these gifts were worthless. The monthly prize may have been of modest financial value but had huge symbolic value. It was public recognition for achievement. If you are going to give for free, give well. If you give and do a shoddy job, people will remember the shoddy job rather than your generosity. You will lose influence rather than gain it.

Measured Generosity

Giving your best is true in terms of quality but not in terms of quantity. The more you give, the less it is valued. If we give and continue to give unconditionally, we can quickly become exploited.

Measured generosity requires clarity about who to help, how to help, and how much to help. That means learning to say no to requests for help. This can feel awkward, but it is far better to say no than commit to doing something and doing it poorly. Poor work destroys your credibility.

There are three principles to saying no gracefully:

1. Be clear about your decision.
2. Be clear and honest about why you cannot do it.
3. If possible, offer an alternative.

Let me give you an example: I sometimes deliver project management presentations internationally and I love to do it because I meet many new people. More and more frequently, people expect to receive copies of my books for free. I do it sometimes but not as the rule. I cannot understand why some people ask me to do that. Writing a book requires knowledge, time, and a lot of effort. I can give a couple of books as a gift, applying my generosity. But people should not expect to receive my books for free. If you don't value your time and effort, you will destroy your career step by step.

I strongly believe that people need to be compensated in some way. Generosity has a limit and need to be measured. When you give everything people cannot appreciate the value of what you have given them.

I made many mistakes in my professional life regarding generosity and I'm still doing it. I strongly recommend you to learn to say no in those occasions.

Requested Help

The only help people value is the help they ask for. If they don't ask, don't give. It can be difficult to resist the temptation, especially if you see a team member struggling or going in the wrong direction. They'll learn more from experience than from some unasked-for interference, however well meaning it is. If they are too shy or too proud to ask for help, an innocent "How's it going?" as you pass their desk should be enough to prompt the request. In my experience, young and inexperienced people are usually shy, so you need to facilitate and create a good and healthy atmosphere.

I have experience mentoring people in a multinational organization. Some managers assigned me as a mentor to project managers, but those project managers never requested a mentor, so it did not work.

I was lucky because one junior project manager requested my help. I started to work with him as his mentor. After six months he spoke well about my help and support to the rest of the organization. Word of mouth helped me in that particular case. Other project managers started to ask for a mentor. From then on, the mentor role was more valuable for that organization.

Five Characteristics of the Generous Project Manager

Although there are many different types of generous people, there are some common traits that the most generous people share.

Whether they give their time or their money, the individuals most devoted to giving back to their communities and families largely share these qualities.

Although the Latin root of the word generous means "of noble birth," by no means is generosity limited to people in positions of power. While it is typically high-profile people who are in the news for their generosity, anyone can become more generous simply by paying attention to one's actions. In the case of the project manager he or she may use generosity to influence project stakeholders using the characteristics described in the following sections.

Altruism

First and foremost, generous project managers are altruistic. They give without hopes of receiving compensation for their good deeds. Personal gain may occur, but it is not a motivating factor for the most generous project manager. For 21 years I have belonged to the PMI (Project Management Institute) and I like sharing my best practices and experience with other members without expecting anything in return. Likewise, most of PMI members do the same.

One of my best practices is spending some personal time with my team members when managing a project. In that way I have the opportunity to offer to help with any issues they have and to clarify personal and project expectations with them. I am investing part of my free time on it, but I believe it to be worthwhile.

One good example is an information technology (IT) project I managed for the Ministry of Works in Spain. In that project I had a team of 25 people, but 20 of them were young and inexperienced people. I was pressed because I needed to achieve my project objectives on time, on cost, and within schedule. Then I gave part of my free time to my young team members every day when the journey was finished. I spent time with them about the need for asking questions to clarify assignments, and about the importance of teamwork and collaboration. Using my generosity they felt that I cared of them. So little by little they felt much more integrated into the team. Their learning progress was faster than expected.

Optimism

Generous project managers are idealists. They have a certain image of the way the project management world should be and strive to achieve that end. Although the world is not a perfect place, these people do not stop giving their time, energy, or money. As optimists, they see the world in a different light than others.

I consider myself as an optimistic professional, so I truly believe that the world, although not perfect, can be made into a much better place. Then I always try to improve my attitude managing projects being positive and optimistic with all my project stakeholders. My positive attitude creates a positive climate for teamwork and collaboration among team. When the project workload is high, that optimism helps the team to move forward and to work the extra mile. Optimism is a way of influencing people in a positive way.

Trust

Trust is a major quality among the most generous project managers. They completely believe that their cause is a worthy one, and they trust that the people involved with that cause will do their best to help achieve the goal. Trusty people give the benefit of the doubt to everybody. They believe in their people. They do not fail when they have a commitment. They are very supportive with their people and that way they earn their trust. Trusty people are people who care for their team members and peers. For those who give, this means a trust that the others involved with the cause appropriately use their time and resources. Trust is the path for achieving credibility by which you improve your influence skills. Because credibility is gained through a set of details, a trusty person is showing to the rest of the people that he or she cares. So trusty people are good influencers; they are people who continue behaving the same in any circumstances.

Energy

When you think of project managers being generous, energy is one of the first things that come to mind. These professionals devote their energy to the good that they want to do. They also gain energy from their cause. When the most generous people spend their time working on a goal, they are revitalized and energized to do even more good. For example:

I managed a project to run a Spanish national event in Madrid two years ago. I recruited six team members who belonged to the three current PMI Spanish chapters. I always had in my mind to make that event happen in Spain. We needed it in our community. At the beginning of the project were obstacles (e.g., lack of sponsorship, lack of team members' time, lack of money, lack of commitment from some of the members). I needed to make an extra effort because it was a PMI project and nobody would be paid for that. So we needed to have meetings on the weekends. However, that difficulty generated in me more desire to do it. And it was what I transmitted to my team: We can do it. So we prepared a project plan through several meetings, we identified our keynote speakers, we decided on the location, and then we found a sponsor. Everything was ready: BBVA (a Spanish bank) agreed to be our sponsor and then we were ready to do our "call for papers," inviting participants to submit papers. However, one week before starting our call for papers, our sponsor called to resign. Far from despairing, I met my team and I told them: "OK, why don't we try it again by next year?" I expected to get a no as their answer, but they told me: "Alfonso, it is only because of the energy you spent with all the team, that you can count on us." We have restarted all the activities now and our plan is to make it happen by the end of 2014.

Ability to Lead

This quality might seem to be an odd one at first, but the most generous project managers are not afraid to stand up and lead their cause. Although not everyone can actually lead their group or cause, this does not discount these individuals' leadership ability. Getting involved is in itself a form of leadership.

The most generous people share these qualities to differing degrees. If you are concerned with increasing your own level of generosity, these factors can get you started in the right direction.

Philosophy and Principles of Generosity

I asked the following question to several project managers worldwide: What has helped you to grow most in your life as a project manager? Several common themes emerged. Project managers said things like:

"I had someone who encouraged me."
"They gave me time and made me feel the center of their world."
"They focused on what I did well but were also prepared to tell the truth."
"They were generous and helped me to follow my way."

More recently I have asked people about how they learned to be generous. Some talk about parents, friends, teachers, managers, leaders, and others who embodied the spirit of generosity. Some talk about growing up in a certain culture—a school, a team, or a workplace—that encouraged people to develop and also give to others. Some talk about learning it from spiritual or religious traditions.

Some people talk about critical points in their lives when they chose to be generous rather than—in its widest sense—greedy. They found that being caring led to both them and others feeling better.

Summary

Generosity is the art of taking by giving that creates a reciprocal relationship among people. Generosity contributes to developing your influence as a project manager. It is not like being Father Christmas and distributing presents in the pursuit of popularity. Leaders do not need to be popular. They need to be trusted and respected. The search for popularity leads to weakness and a cycle of ever-growing expectations. Building trust builds commitment and loyalty, which are better lasting than popularity.

Generosity in the project management world is about giving the scarcest resource of all. The scarcest resource in management is not money, it is time. Being generous with personal time appears to be suicidal when there are so many day-to-day pressures to meet. But by creating a network of alliances, mutual obligations, and debts that can be called in, the influencer invests heavily in the future. It is an investment that saves time and raises performance in the longer term. Generosity is a habit that can be acquired. It is not just profitable to give, it is also enjoyable.

Generosity Assessment

Following are several statements that address how you may or may not relate to other people in your life. Please indicate your level of agreement with the following statements in terms of how well they describe you. Use 1 for strongly disagree to 6 for strongly agree.

QUESTION	SCORE
1. When one of my team members needs my attention, I really try to slow down and give them the time and help they need.	_____
2. I am known by team members and colleagues as someone who makes time to pay attention to others' problems.	_____
3. I'm the kind of person who is willing to go the "extra mile" to help take care of my team members, project stakeholders, and friends.	_____
4. When team members or colleagues experience something upsetting or discouraging, I make a special point of being kind to them.	_____
5. When it comes to my personal relationships with others, I am a very generous person.	_____
6. It makes me very happy to be a giver in ways that meet their needs.	_____
7. It is just as important to me that other people around me are happy and thriving as it is that I am happy and thriving.	_____
8. My decisions are often based on concern for the welfare of others.	_____
9. I am usually willing to risk my own feelings being hurt in the process if I stand a chance of helping someone else in need.	_____
10. I make it a point to let my friends and family know how much I love, want, and need them.	_____

Note: For each assessment, there is a scoring algorithm leading to one of three acuity ranges: low, moderate, or high. Each item is scored 1 to 6, as indicated earlier. The possible range for the sum total of all 10 items is 10 to 60.

Reverse Scores: None

Algorithm

    10–46 Low generosity

    47–56 Moderate generosity

    57–60 High generosity

7

UNDERSTANDING PEOPLE

Understand people and it will be easier for you to influence them.

Alfonso Bucero

The ability to understand people is one of the greatest assets anyone can ever have. It has the potential to positively impact every area of your life, not just the business arena. If you are not able to understand people, then you will not be able to influence them. You need to know what their worries are, what do they expect from you, and what are their expectations and desires. Then you will have the possibility to influence them.

Understanding people certainly impacts your ability to communicate with others. The biggest mistake I made in the past was to frequently put my highest priority on expressing my ideas and feelings. What most people really want is to be listened to, respected, and understood. The moment people see that they are being understood, they become more motivated to understand your points of view. If you can learn to understand people, how they think, what they feel, what inspires them, and how they are likely to act and react in a given situation, then you can motivate and influence them in a positive way.

Then, in order to influence people we need to consider what is best: to be loved or feared. Machiavelli pondered that timeless conundrum five hundred years ago and hedged his bets. Machiavelli poses a basic question that all politicians have to answer for themselves: Is it better to be loved than feared or feared than loved? And his answer is clear: Fear is better. "Upon this a question arises: whether it be better to be loved than feared or feared than loved? One should wish to be both, but, because it is difficult to unite them in one person, it is much safer to be feared than loved."

Safer is better, too, because you won't have to watch your back as much. People will be less likely to conspire against someone they fear than someone they love. Now behavioral research is weighing in with research showing that Machiavelli had it partly right: When we judge others—especially our leaders—we look first at two characteristics: how lovable they are (their warmth, communion, or trustworthiness) and how fearsome they are (their strength or competence).

Why are these traits so important? Because they answer two critical questions: (1) What are this person's intentions toward me? (2) Is he or she capable of acting on those intentions? Together these assessments underlie our emotional and behavioral reactions to other people, groups, and even brands and companies. Research by Amy Cuddy, Susan Fiske, and Peter Glick, of Lawrence University (*Harvard Business Review*, 2013) shows that people judged to be competent but lacking in warmth often elicit envy in others, an emotion involving respect and resentment that cuts both ways. When we respect someone, we want to cooperate or affiliate ourselves with him or her, but resentment can make that person vulnerable to harsh reprisal.

A person judged as warm but incompetent tends to elicit pity, which also involves a mix of emotions. Compassion moves us to help those we pity, but our lack of respect leads us ultimately to neglect them (think of workers who become marginalized as they are near retirement or of an employee with outmoded skills in a rapidly evolving industry).

Insights from the field of psychology show that these two dimensions account for more than 90% of the variance in our positive or negative impressions we form of the people around us. So which is better: being lovable or being strong? Most leaders today tend to emphasize their strength, competence, and credentials in the workplace, but that is exactly the wrong approach in my opinion, because in order to influence people you need to listen to them first.

Why People Fail to Understand Others

Lack of understanding concerning others is a recurrent source of stress in our society. If understanding is such an asset, why don't more people practice it? There are many reasons.

Fear

When people do not understand others, they rarely try to overcome their fear in order to learn more about them. It becomes a vicious cycle.

Unfortunately, fear is evident in the workplace when it comes to employees' reactions toward their leaders. Laborers fear their managers. Middle managers are intimidated by senior managers. Both groups are sometimes afraid of executives. The whole situation causes undue suspicion, lack of communication, and reduced productivity. Fear can undermine cognitive potential, creativity, and problem solving, and cause employees to get stuck and even disengage. It is a "hot" emotion, with long-lasting effects. It burns into our memory in a way that cooler emotions do not.

I strongly believe that warmth is the conduit of influence. It facilitates trust and communication and absorption of ideas. There are many signs from your body language that can show people that you are pleased to be in their company. When warmth is your priority it helps you connect immediately with those around you, demonstrating that you hear them, understand them, and can be trusted by them.

For example, when I was working on IT (information technology) projects in banking organizations, I observed the following behaviors from project managers:

- They think their ideas will be rejected.
- They feel colleagues won't like the ideas.
- They think they won't get credit if the ideas work.
- They are afraid the boss will be threatened by the ideas.
- They are concerned that they will be labeled as troublemakers.
- They are afraid of losing their jobs if they suggest ideas that do not work.

In my opinion if you give the others the benefit of the doubt and replace fear with understanding, everyone can work together positively.

Self-Centeredness

There are two sides to every question as long as it does not concern us personally. One way to overcome our natural self-centeredness is to try to see things from other people's perspectives. For instance,

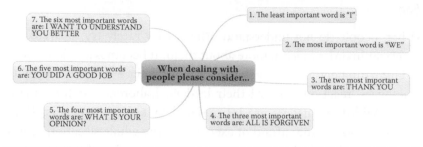

Figure 7.1   Considerations when dealing with people.

the salesperson's challenge is to see the world from the customer's viewpoint. And I believe it is the challenge for every one of us as project managers.

When dealing with other people, consider the statements shown in Figure 7.1.

Changing your attitude from self-centeredness to understanding requires desire and commitment to always try to see things from the other person's point of view.

Not Appreciating Differences

We need to respect and recognize everyone else's unique qualities. Learning to appreciate their differences is the right path in my personal experience. If somebody in your team has a talent that you don't have, great. The two of you can strengthen each other's weaknesses. For instance, I used to work with people from different cultures and I consider myself as a lucky person because of that. You need to celebrate people's differences in temperament. Variety makes for interesting dynamics between people. People from different cultures see things from a different perspective, from a different angle. Changing the frame of reference is usually helpful because it obliges you to reflect upon something in a different way.

For instance, my wife works with me on the same project in our small company. She is very analytic and pragmatic; she knows how to take care of all the small details when we are preparing a project proposal for a customer. I am much more a dreamer and visionary. So that mix works well for us, because it is a good combination. The combination of differences has helped us when presenting solution proposals to customers and we influenced them to be convinced of our solution.

Not Acknowledging Similarities

As much as you know more about people and get to know others, you begin to realize that people have a lot in common. We all have hopes and fears, joys and sorrows, victories, and problems. A clear example is the first Project Management Institute (PMI) Congress I attended in 1993 in the United States. As soon as I talked to other international colleagues I found they had similar problems and issues with the projects they managed that I had in the projects I managed in Spain.

Most people have an emotional reaction to what's happening around them. To foster understanding, think what your emotions would be if you were in the same position as the person you are inter-acting with. You know what you would want to happen in a given situation. Chances are that the person you are working with has many of the same feelings.

For example, a couple of years ago I directed a master's pro-gram in project management at the Technical University of Madrid (UPM). During the training course, the students were asked to select a project that would be defended at the end of the course. They had the possibility to choose between two teachers as project mentors. One of the teachers always had students lined up waiting to talk to him, while the other had nothing to do. I was curious to know what the reason was because both were good teachers. I asked one student and he told me: The reason is because the teacher who has a long line of students waiting for him listens to everyone and asked everyone to write his or her commitment in a project charter. He cares for the students.

How Do People React to Your Style?

Research by Amy Cuddy (*Harvard Business Review*, July 2013) sug-gests that the way others perceive your levels of warmth and compe-tence determines the emotions you elicit and your ability to influence

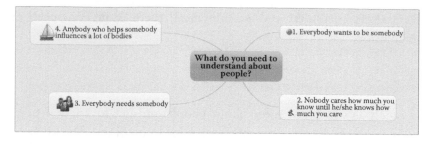

Figure 7.2   What do you need to understand about people?

a situation. For example, if you are highly competent but show only moderate warmth, you will get people to go along with you, but you won't earn their true engagement and support. If you show no warmth, beware of those who may try to derail your efforts and maybe your career.

Some Things Everybody Needs to Understand about People

Knowing what people need and want is the key to understanding them. If you can understand them, you can influence them and impact their lives in a positive way. If we were to boil down all the things we know about understanding people and narrow them down to a short list, we would identify the five things shown in Figure 7.2.

Everybody Wants to Be Somebody

There is not a person in the world who does not have the desire to be someone, to have significance. Even the least ambitious and unassuming person wants to be highly regarded by others. Let me give you an example: In 1993 when I attended my first PMI Congress in North America I attended the PMI Awards Ceremony. I was really impacted by the public recognition that PMI gave to some professionals. The large audience in the room was spectacular. I dreamed to be up there some day. Nineteen years later that happened.

It is funny how that kind of dream can impact your life. Everybody wants to be regarded and valued by others. In other words, everybody wants to be somebody. Once that piece of information becomes a part of your everyday thinking, you will gain incredible insight into why people do the things they do. If you treat every person you meet as if he or she were the most important person in the world, you will communicate that he or she is somebody to you.

Nobody Cares How Much You Know until He or She Knows How Much You Care

If you want to be a project manager with influence you need to love people before you try to lead them. The moment that people know that you care for and about them, the way they feel about you changes.

Showing others that you care is not always easy. I believe the greatest times and fondest memories will come because of people, but so will your most difficult, hurtful, and tragic times. People are your greatest assets and your greater liabilities. The challenge is to keep caring about them no matter what.

- People are illogical, unreasonable, and self-centered; love them anyway.
- If you do good, people will accuse you of selfish ulterior motives; do good.
- If you are successful, you will win false friends and true enemies; succeed anyway.
- The good you do today will perhaps be forgotten tomorrow; do good anyway.
- Honesty and frankness make you vulnerable; be honest and frank anyway.
- The biggest man with the biggest ideas can be shot down by the smallest man with the smallest mind; think big anyway.
- People favor underdogs but follow only big dogs; fight for the few underdogs anyway.
- What you spend years building may be destroyed overnight; build anyway.
- People really need help but may attack you if you help them; help them anyway.
- Give the world the best that you have and you will get kicked in the teeth; give the world the best that you have anyway.

If better is possible, then good is not enough. If you want to help others and become a person of influence, keep smiling, sharing, giving, and turning the other cheek. That's the right way to treat people.

Everybody Needs Somebody

Everybody needs friendship, encouragement, and help. What people can accomplish by themselves is nothing compared to their potential when working with others. Doing things with other people tends to bring contentment. For example: When I manage projects I always encourage my team members to share what they did during the week with the other team members. In that way I try to demonstrate that exchanging experiences and thoughts can avoid reinventing the wheel and they need each other to continue working in the project in order to achieve their objectives. Asking questions and sharing ideas is always helpful. People who try to do everything alone often get themselves into trouble.

Everybody Can Be Somebody

Once you understand people and believe in them, they really can become somebody. And it does not take much effort to help other people feel important. Little things, done deliberately at the right time, can make a big difference. For example: At the beginning of my professional career I started working in Fujitsu Spain as an engineer, and I made many mistakes when trying to accomplish my assignments. Little by little I corrected my mistakes and I was very lucky because I had a manager who met me every Friday afternoon for at least ten minutes and reinforced what I accomplished well that week. He made me feel happy and he encouraged me to move forward.

Anybody Who Helps Somebody Influences a Lot of People

The final thing you need to understand about people is that when you help one person, you are really impacting a lot of other people. What you give to one person overflows into the lives of all the people that person impacts. The nature of influence is to multiply. It even impacts you because when you help others and your reasons are good, you always receive more than you can ever give. Most people are so genuinely grateful when another person makes them feel that they are somebody special, that they never tire of showing their gratitude.

The Ability to Understand People

Finally, the ability to understand people is a choice. It is true that some people are born with great instincts that enable them to understand how others think and feel. But even if you are not an instinctive person, you can improve your ability to work with others. Every person is capable of having the ability to understand, motivate, and ultimately influence others.

The Other Person's Perspective

Whenever you look at things from the other person's perspective, you will receive a whole new way of looking at life. And you will find other ways of helping others. The following story provides an example.

A king was upset because his favorite dog was missing. The king sent couriers throughout the land to look for it, but without any successful result. In desperation, the king offered a great reward. Many came hoping to win it and searched for the dog, but they all failed. The dog had disappeared. A simpleton at the king's court sought an audience with the monarch and told him that he could find the dog.

"You," exclaimed the king. "You can find my dog when all others have failed?"

"Yes, sire," answered the simpleton.

"OK, do it," said the king, who had nothing to lose. Within hours the dog was back at the palace, and the king was astonished. He immediately had his treasurer issue a handsome reward to the man and asked him to explain how he had found the dog when many men considered wise had not.

"It was easy, sire," said the simpleton. "I merely asked myself, 'If I were a dog where would I go?' And putting myself in his place, I soon found him."

Personal Empathy

Another quality that you need to develop if you want to understand others is personal empathy. Not everyone is naturally empathetic, that is, not all the people are able to put themselves in other people's boots. People have problems and issues, and those problems affect their reactions. So you need to understand that people's reactions are not always negative because they are their natural response but because they have a special reason.

Positive Attitude about People

People usually see what they look for and hear what they listen for. If you have a positive attitude about people, believe the best of them, and act on your beliefs, then you can have an impact on their lives. But it all starts with the way you think of others. You cannot be a positive influencer if your thinking is negative. Your attitude toward people is one of the most important choices you will ever make. If your thinking is positive, you can really make an impact on them.

If you want to become a person of influence, have a positive attitude toward others. If you treat every person you meet as if he or she were the most important person in the world, you communicate that he or she is somebody to you.

To make an impact on others, find out what people want and then help them to get it. That's what motivates them. And that's what makes it possible for you to become a person of influence in their lives.

Projecting Warmth

When professionals want to project warmth, they sometimes increase the enthusiasm in their voice, increasing their volume and dynamic range to convey delight. That can be effective in the right setting, but if those around you have done nothing in particular to earn your adulation, they will assume either that you're faking or that you fawn over everyone indiscriminately. See the image of a woman projecting warmth in Figure 7.3.

A better way to create vocal warmth is to speak with lower pitch and volume, as you would if you were comforting a friend. Aim for a tone that suggests that you are leveling with people, that you are sharing the straight scoop, with no pretense or emotional adornment. In doing so, you signal that you trust those you are talking with to handle things the right way. You might even occasionally share a personal

Figure 7.3 Projecting warmth. (Fotolia image #59224472, ©Antonioguillem/Fotolia.)

story—one that feels private but not inappropriate—in a confiding tone of voice to demonstrate that you are being forthcoming and open. Let's suppose that you want to establish a bond with new employees you are meeting for the first time. You might offer something personal right off the bat, such as recalling how you felt at a similar point in your career. That's often enough to set a congenial tone.

Before people decide what they think of your message, they decide what they think of you. If you show your employees that you hold roughly the same worldview they do, you demonstrate not only empathy but, in their eyes, common sense. So if you want colleagues to listen and agree with you, first agree with them.

For example, imagine that your company is undergoing a reorganization project and your team is feeling deep anxiety over what the change could mean—for quality, innovation, and job security. Acknowledge people's fear and concerns when you speak to them, whether in formal meetings or during water cooler chats. Look them in the eye and say, "I know everybody's feeling a lot of uncertainty right now, and it is unsettling." People will respect you for addressing the elephant in the room and will be more open to hearing what you have to say.

Smiling is important. When we smile sincerely, the warmth becomes self-reinforcing. I mean feeling happy makes us smile, and smiling makes us happy. This facial feedback is also contagious. We tend to mirror one another's nonverbal expressions and emotions, so when we see someone beaming and emanating genuine warmth, we cannot resist smiling, too. Warmth is not easy to fake, of course, and a polite smile fools no one. To project warmth, you have to genuinely feel it. A natural smile, for instance, involves not only the muscles around the mouth but also those around the eyes.

So how do you produce a natural smile? Find some reason to feel happy wherever you may be, even if you have to resort to laughing at your predicament. Introverts in social settings can single out one person to focus on. This can help you channel the sense of comfort you feel with close friends or family. There is one thing to avoid: smiling with your eyebrows raised at anyone over the age of five. This suggests that you are overly eager to please and be liked. It also signals anxiety, which, like warmth, is contagious. It will cost you much more in strength than you will gain in warmth.

Projecting Strength

Strength or competence can be established by virtue of the position you hold, your reputation, and your actual performance. But your presence or behavior always counts, too. The way you carry yourself does not establish your skill level, of course, but it is taken as strong evidence of your attitude, that is, how serious you are and how determined you are to tackle a challenge, which is an important component of overall strength. The trick is to cultivate a demeanor of strength without seeming menacing.

Warmth may be harder to fake, but confidence is harder to talk yourself into. Feeling like an impostor is very common. But self-doubt completely undermines your ability in project confidence, enthusiasm, and passion, the qualities that make up presence. In fact, if you see yourself as an impostor, others will, too. Feeling in command and confident is about connecting with you. And when we are connected with ourselves, it is much easier to connect with others.

Holding your body in certain ways may help. Although we refer to these postures as power poses, they don't increase your dominance over others. They are about personal power. It is hard to overstate the importance of good posture in projecting authority and an intention to be taken seriously. Good posture does not mean the exaggerated chest-out pose known in the military as standing at attention, or raising one's chin up high. It just means reaching your full height, using your muscles to straighten the S-curve in your spine rather than slouching. It sounds trivial, but maximizing the physical space your body takes up makes a substantial difference in how your audience reacts to you, regardless of your height.

If you want to influence people effectively, you have to get the warmth competence dynamic right. Being calm and confident creates space to be warm, open, and appreciative; to choose to act in ways that reflect and express your values and priorities. Once you establish your warmth, your strength is received as a welcome reassurance. Your leadership becomes not a threat but a gift.

Summary

- Understanding people certainly impacts your ability to communicate with others and the way of influencing them. If you are not able to understand people, you will not be able to influence them. You need to know what their worries are, what they expect from you, and their expectations and desires.
- When people do not understand others, they rarely try to overcome their fear in order to learn more about them. It becomes a vicious cycle. This is why it is very important to develop your listening skills.
- There are two sides to every question as long as it does not concern us personally. One way to overcome our natural self-centeredness is to try to see things from other people's perspectives. Changing your attitude from self-centeredness to understanding requires desire and commitments to always try to see things from the other person's point of view.
- We need to respect and recognize everyone else's unique qualities. Learning to appreciate their differences is the right path in my personal experience. If somebody in your team has a talent that you don't have, great. The two of you can strengthen each other's weaknesses.
- The more you know about people and get to know others well, you begin to realize that people have a lot in common. We all have hopes and fears, joys and sorrows, victories, and problems.

- Knowing what people need and want is the key to understanding them. If you can understand them, you can influence them and impact their lives in a positive way.
- Every person is capable of having the ability to understand, motivate, and ultimately influence others.

Understanding People Checklist

- Rate your understanding—Use the following scale to rate your ability to understand people.
  - Superior—I always anticipate how people will feel and react in any given situation. Understanding is one of my strongest abilities.
  - Good—Most of the time what people do and want make sense to me. I consider my ability to understand people an asset.
  - Fair—I am surprised by people just as often as I am able to anticipate their thinking. I consider my ability to understand others to be average.
  - Poor—Most of the time people's feelings and motivations are mysteries to me. I definitely need to do better in this area.
- Understanding action plan—If you rated yourself superior, then you should be sharing your skill by teaching others how to better understand people. If you rated yourself good, fair, or poor, keep striving to learn and improve. You can improve your ability immediately by asking yourself the following questions:
  - Where did they come from?
  - Where do they want to go?
  - What is their need now?
  - How can I help?
- Activate your positive attitude—If your ability to understand people is not as good as you would like to be, the root cause may be that you don't value others as highly as you could. As you interact with people, remember the words of Ken Keyes: "A loving person lives in a loving world. A hostile person lives in a hostile world." Everyone you meet is your mirror.

8

DEVELOP COMMITMENT

Persuasion encourages someone to do something once. Influence is about encouraging them to keep on doing something and to keep on supporting you. It lasts and is based on voluntary commitment. Influence is the gift that keeps on giving. There are ways of persuading people to do something once. It can be even harder to persuade the same person a second time, because this time he or she will be more cautious. However, if you have influenced someone well, he or she will keep returning to you time and again. Persuasion is a quick fix; influence is the lasting solution.

At the heart of the commitment process is reciprocity. You should give and take at every stage. The most common mistakes in building commitment come from ignoring this principle. The typical errors are:

1. Expecting too much too soon—Don't ask to marry someone within five minutes of meeting him or her; you are unlikely to get lucky. The commitment process is incremental. You have to build trust slowly on both sides. Start with the small requests before you get to the big requests.
2. Giving but not taking—The urge to impress can be bad. We want to make a good impression, so we keep on giving. And then we get taken for granted; we become a slave, not a partner. It is very hard to change that relationship once the expectations have been set.
3. Taking but not giving—We meet the important person, ask for their help, and get it. Delighted, we ask for another favor later, and another, and another. And then suddenly we find we can no longer meet the important person. Everybody finally expects something in return, and if that return never happens, then they are not ready to give anymore.

Be patient; take your time, give and take. Become the trusted partner. This is a different mind-set from the crude world of persuasion, which is all about doing a deal now and moving on to the next sucker fast. Influencers are playing for bigger stakes with longer lasting rewards.

Building influence requires commitment, from both sides. You are building a partnership. The challenge is to become the trusted partner of a stranger. They do not know you, but they want your support. There are some elements to the commitment process:

1. The hook
2. Making commitment a two-way street
3. Using territory well
4. Building a tribe: Belonging, meaning, and recognition
5. Gaining commitment by giving control
6. Public commitment, private challenge

Many of us spend most of our time building influence with people we already know. If you are in this happy position, you can skip the first step (the hook).

The Hook

Most journeys fail not because of storms along the way, but because we never find the time, opportunity, or courage to start out in the first place. The hardest step is the first step. And this is true of influencing. How do we influence someone we have never met? Why will they choose to meet us?

This first step is hard because:

- We may not know what the right sort of hook is for our target.
- Our target may be hard to access, behind protective secretaries.
- Few of us actually enjoy cold calling. We need courage and a few techniques to help us.

There are three established hooks that work for me:

1. Personal introductions
2. The teaser
3. Asking for advice

To explain how the hook works, I will share with you an example: I wanted to start a subsidiary of my company in Dubai. That requires at least $500,000 of capital. I checked my bank account. I was at least $400,000 short of the required capital. So I needed to find a partner. That means I needed to talk to the CEOs of some companies. Not only did I not have enough money, but my contacts book was completely devoid of CEOs. I needed a hook to get them interested.

Personal Introductions

The first step was to find some personal introductions. This is where the Six Degrees of Kevin Bacon game is helpful. Kevin Bacon is a film star. The game proposes that no one is more than six degrees of separation away from him. The BBC put this game to the test in 2009. They gave 40 parcels to people around the world. The goal was to get the parcel to a scientist in Boston, by passing the parcel on to someone they already knew on first-name basis who they thought might be closer to the scientist. From the depths of rural Kenya and elsewhere, it took on average six steps to reach that scientist. However, of the 40 packages that the BBC started with, only three made it to the final destination. That sums up the nature of targeted networking. We may only be six steps away from the person we want to meet, but knowing which six steps to take is very hard. In my case I was successful on some occasions using my network contacts. I took care of creating my network several years ago and I try to maintain it by contacting people from time to time.

We can expect to set out in the wrong direction more than nine times out of ten. The journey may be short, but it is not easy. Persistence is required. We live in a small world. If we work at it, we can find a way through to anyone we need to find.

The Teaser

Even with a personal introduction, it made sense to strengthen the hook with a problem solution offer. The problem solution offer is the staple of much advertising: our product relieves headaches faster, or our computers are more lightweight and powerful. We may dislike such advertising, but it works. We have a problem and the advertising offers a solution. To be really effective, the pitch should be personal. So the next step was a short letter that looked like this:

Dear XXXX:

I am writing on the advice of John Jones who thought it might be of mutual benefit for us to explore a new business proposal. We are developing a branch of our company in your area, which can fill a gap in your portfolio between your successful SME and corporate business. We expect your company to achieve $50 million pretax profits within five years.

I represent a group of senior consultants who have been developing this proposal and can form the start-up team to bring this idea to market fast.

In the first instance, it will make sense for us to have an exploratory discussion to see if this idea fits with your current portfolio and priorities. I will call your secretary next week to arrange a suitable time to meet you.

Yours truly,

XXXX

No hook letter is perfect, and it does not need to be. It simply needs to work. The aforementioned letter worked as a hook. Note that it was a letter, not an e-mail. E-mails are deleted faster than letters hit the wastebasket. The letter shows you have made an effort and there is a chance that it will be read and remembered. The principles behind the letter also apply to a phone pitch or any other initial contact where you need to hook someone into an initial meeting. The main principles behind the hook in the letter are numbered and explained in the following:

1. This is the personal introduction, right up front to grab attention. The CEO knew and respected John Jones (an example). The goal was to stop the secretary from immediately putting the letter in the wastebasket. Whether writing or speaking, you need to get past the first sentence. A weak first sentence leads to switch off.
2. Note the positive verbs. Not "might" or "hoping to" or "thinking about." We are doing it, the only question is who with: If

you refuse, your archrivals may decide to be a partner instead. Project confidence, not uncertainty.

3. Be very clear about what the idea is, so they see it is specific and they understand it.

4. Make it highly personalized to this organization; be positive about its existing portfolio, otherwise you will encourage a defensive reaction and denial.

5. Size the prize. It is worth the CEO getting out of bed? It is not something for a junior analyst to look into? Does it answer the question: Why should I bother?

6. Be credible. Show there is support, momentum, and commitment. In truth, the senior bankers were interested but were not going to give up their day jobs until a deal was done. This answers the question: Do I believe what is being said?

7. This is an easy task: invest an hour of your time to see if you want to obtain millions a year. This is the first step of incremental commitment.

8. The CEO will not read this letter, the secretary will. Promise to follow up. When you follow up, the secretary will have forgotten about or ignored your letter, so be ready to resend it. Second time around, the secretary will take it seriously because he or she now knows you will follow up, so he or she will show the letter to the CEO and ask for advice. The hardest task can be getting past the switchboard to the secretary.

9. Keep it short. The more you write, the more there is for them to disagree with or dislike.

Ask for Advice

There is an even easier, and often better, way of hooking people. Instead of offering them something, ask for something. The one thing people are normally happy to give is advice. By giving advice it shows that our judgment is valued and that we have some expertise and knowledge about the subject in question. By asking for advice, we flatter someone. Let me share an example: Some years ago I was working for a multinational organization and, when managing a big IT customer project for a bank organization, I asked for some advice from my manager about managing customer relationships. I needed to work together with him because he would be the contact for the customer project sponsor, and I had some obstacles to overcome to make that project successful. My personal relationship with him was not fantastic, but as soon as I asked him for advice, my relationship positively changed. I worked with him for two years and I understood the power of asking for advice can have in terms of influence.

Within a firm, most senior managers are delighted to give people the benefit of their wisdom. It costs them little and reinforces their self-image as respected, important, and knowledgeable people. Asking for advice gently exploits the vanity of managers and leads to a more productive conversation than daring to offer advice. The curse of smart people is that they like to show they are smart. Really smart people have the self-confidence to avoid this trap and to appear humble.

If you ask for advice, ask early. Asking for advice is not just about flattering egos. It also works because you give your colleague a sense of control and influence over the outcome. If they control the outcome, they own it. People rarely oppose something that they feel they own and control. The later you leave the request for advice, the less influence your colleague has over the outcome and the less commitment they will feel toward it. Asking for advice early, and keep on asking for it. Share ownership of the final result with anyone who can either derail or endorse the outcome.

Making Commitment a Two-Way Street

Commitment is a two-way street but is often treated as a one-way street. The goal of the commitment process is to achieve trusted-partner status. A trusted partner will work with you as equals toward a common goal. If you are to be equals and you are both to work together, you have to establish that mind-set from the outset. This is commonly missed. Some people demand commitment and others give commitment without reciprocating. One-way commitments are not healthy and fail to achieve influence.

All of this is obvious, but as George Orwell wrote, "Seeing what is in front of your nose requires constant struggle." The goal is obvious, but many people are unaware of it. And achieving the goal is far harder than stating it. In many cases, commitment ends up a one-way street.

Most firms have a few egotists who believe commitment is all one-way. For them, being a team player means "you accept my orders or you are not on my team." This also means giving orders and blame, while taking all the credit. These are rarely pleasant relationships, except for the egotist who is very happy with the way the world revolves around him or her.

The more common one-way street is where we ourselves are making all the commitment. This is where we play into the hands of the egotists and the merely idle. In our desire to impress and show how good we are, we work harder and harder to show what we can do. We end up in a very dysfunctional relationship. Each time we impress, we simply raise expectations. That forces us to work harder than ever, and we get nothing in return. We have not created a partnership of influence; we have turned ourselves into willing slaves. Influence is based on a partnership of mutual commitment and obligation.

Creating mutual commitment has to start from the first meeting. The longer you leave it, the harder it is to change the nature of the relationship. In practice, this means you have to ask for something even from the first meeting. It may only be a token effort, but it sets the tone and the expectations going forward. Here are some simple things I have asked clients to do for me after first meetings:

- Forward a link to an article that the client mentioned.
- Clarify a small piece of data that we discussed.
- Check, and report, on the views of two colleagues.

These are small tasks that are a big first step. Your partner has made the vital transition from being passive to being active. As a passive counterpart they do little more than act as judge and jury. But they are not helping you perform. They are spectators, not partners and you have little influence over them. By making them into active partners, even in a small way, you have set the relationship onto a far more productive path.

As soon as your client or colleague has done some homework for you, they have established a platform for building two-way commitment. You are now in a position to praise and thank them for their work. Giving praise is a power position. By giving praise you have evened up what may have started as an unequal relationship. You have also created the excuse for reciprocating with a favor of your own and for exploring more ideas. The one-way street is becoming a two-way street, but you need to push this new psychological contract further.

At an early stage, set up a meeting away from the client's home territory. "Early" means the second meeting. When the client or colleague is in their office they are on their territory. You are the visitor that they have allowed in, and they are the gracious host. The guest–visitor relationship is not a partnership. You need to break that mind-set fast. Find an excuse to meet on your territory or on neutral territory. Once they have moved out of their territory, the nature of the relationship changes. The conversation can change from what you will do for them. You migrate more easily to the partnership model where you can start to have real influence.

Using Territory Well

Human beings are territorial. We all mark our territory. We all tend to feel more comfortable in our home territory than in the alien world of a boardroom or the office of a customer or senior executive.

People use different scripts based on the territory they are in. The most basic script is the ask–give script. Usually, when you go to someone else's territory you are asking them for something. When they come to you, they are asking you for something. The asker has to do all the hard work, while the giver sits as judge and jury deciding whether to give and if so on what terms. This does not promote influencing; influence is about creating a partnership of equals, which does not come from an ask–give script. The easiest way to get a partnership script is to find neutral territory. On neutral territory, ask–give scripts quickly disappear. So the question is how to get onto neutral territory as fast as possible. The answer: ask someone out. It may be as simple as getting breakfast together before work or agreeing to have lunch in the cafeteria together.

Or it can be as elaborate as corporate entertaining. On neutral territory the conversation changes. You have the chance to talk socially, to discover mutual interests, and build rapport. Any business discussion more naturally becomes a partnership discussion rather than an ask–give discussion. You build relationships better over pasta than over PowerPoint.

The territory principle helps corporate entertaining work. The vendor is no longer on the buyer's territory. The buyer recognizes that the rules of the game have changed and an entirely different set of conversations happens at the sporting or cultural event. There is a surfeit of corporate entertaining opportunities out there, and the person you want to entertain may well be sick of corporate entertaining. So make sure you find an opportunity that reflects their personal interests. Or find something that will give them bragging rights back at the office.

Building a Tribe: Belonging, Meaning, and Recognition

In many firms loyalty is a one-way street. The firm demands loyalty, passion, and commitment right up to the moment when you are right-sized, downsized, off-shored, best-shored, re-engineered, outsourced, or just plain fired. Unrequited love and unrequited loyalty rarely last long. To sustain commitment, managers need to give as well as take. There are two basic needs any firm or manager must fulfill to generate voluntary commitment:

1. Belonging and meaning
2. Recognition

In my experience, in those cases where employment is at will or secure by law, the manager needs to be focused on creating a healthy environment where trust and confidence are the key. So that way people feel comfortable on a daily basis. In this environment people are not worried about losing their jobs, but they are human beings that need to live in a comfortable environment.

Belonging and Meaning

The tribal instinct runs deep. We all have a need to belong to a group. The desire to belong is universal. The way we dress proclaims our tribe. The corporate tribe has subtle dress codes that vary by type of business, function, level, and occasion. Even rebellious teenagers invest a huge amount of time and money acquiring an identity that allows them to belong to one of the ever-shifting tribes of teenage fashion and music. Fortunately, most managers do not have to go to war or become a teenager again to understand and use the power of belonging and meaning.

The power of belonging sustains loyalty in even the most adverse conditions. Sports fans are a good example. There are organizations that build extraordinary esprit de corps and gain extraordinary commitment from staff. Once people have a sense of belonging, their commitment is voluntary and they become self-policing. They perform not because the boss tells them to. They perform because they do not want to let their colleagues down and they do not want to let themselves down. Peer group pressure is far more intense than boss pressure. Boss pressure is about compliance; peer group pressure is about commitment.

When people have a sense of belonging and meaning, even mundane work becomes meaningful. For example, when working for a multinational organization I was assigned to an internal project that consisted of creating a project management office. I explained to my whole team why we were doing that project. However, when one of my managers asked different team members, their answers were slightly different. My manager asked the first team member, "What are you doing?" and he replied, "I'm choosing some binders to archive the project files." My manager asked the second team member the same question, and he answered, "I'm writing a methodology checklist for project audits." My manager then asked the third team member the same question and he answered, "I'm working in the creation of our PMO to achieve better project and organizational results." The same work can either be made meaningless or meaningful. Make work meaningful and commitment rises.

Recognition

Recognition is a tool that is at the disposal of all influencers. As we look back at the people who have positively influenced us, they are likely to be teachers, parents, or even colleagues and bosses who recognized our talents and forgave our very minor defects. We respond well to recognition. Very few people think that they are overrecognized for their talents and contribution. That is a wonderful opportunity for an influencer. It allows an influencer to fill a void in someone's life to stand out from other people who do not give enough recognition.

Recognition is an art. It can be done poorly or well. Done poorly, it comes across as insincere. One-minute managers who throw around condescending and generic compliments quickly lose credibility. Good praise is specific, personal, and detailed. For example, if someone helps you:

- Explain why the action was useful to you
- Explain what was useful about it, what it achieved

Private recognition is a start; public recognition is even better. It works because it

- Focuses debate on agreements rather than disagreements
- Creates an emotional debt to you from the people being praised
- Forms the impression of a bandwagon that is starting to roll
- Builds support for you
- Reinforces the behavior you want to focus on

Recognition is not just about recognizing people who agree with you. It can be also be used to turn disagreement into agreement. The best way to win an argument is without fighting. Always look for the positive and give praise and recognition. People become less defensive and more open to change once they feel extraordinary talents and effort have been properly recognized.

Gaining Commitment by Giving Control

Management control is seen to be good. Many managers think that control means reporting, measuring, monitoring, assessing, and praising. This is control, but it is alienating because staff members prefer to be trusted than controlled.

There is an alternative to heavy management control: self-control and control through peer pressure. These forms of control are voluntary and lead to a commitment culture instead of a compliance culture. At a basic level, most people want to stay in control of their lives and their jobs. If someone else is controlling us we tend to resent it. Good influencers use the concept of self-control to induce high commitment and high performance.

Giving control is an act of delegation. You can delegate away control, but you cannot delegate away accountability. Managers should always be held accountable. But you can change the nature of your role. You no longer add value by ordering, controlling, measuring, and assessing. You add value by supporting and coaching, clearing political logjams, securing resources, and managing other stakeholders such as top management. In other words, you create a new role where you add real value to the team, instead of simply being another layer of bureaucracy. Delegating control does not destroy management.

Public Commitment, Private Challenge

Public commitments are powerful commitments; they cannot be taken back. For example, I once made a mistake of deciding to run a marathon. I trained, and then realized it was too much. I dropped the idea. Then I made a mistake. I told four colleagues that I would run. They laughed and told everyone else; when challenged, I confirmed I was going to run. Suddenly, I was committed. There was no going back and no excuses. Letting myself down is not great. So I trained and completed the marathon. I will never make the same mistake again.

The principle of public commitment runs both ways. It can be positive or negative. Once a colleague has taken a position in public, he or she finds it very hard to renounce that position.

Manage Conflict in Private

Managing conflict in private is a basic requirement of influence. This is especially important when you have a new idea you want to promote. If you raise your idea in a meeting, say good-bye to your idea. Meetings are designed to kill ideas and to discourage anyone else from daring to have ideas. The last time I made the mistake of having an idea in a meeting, I found myself at the wrong end of a shooting gallery. The bullets all came in the form of helpful questions: How much will it cost? Is it in your budget? Whose budget is it? Who will work on it? This is the normal reaction to new ideas in meetings. Unless you know you have support, keep critical discussions in private.

The dividing line between a private and public meeting is two people. As soon as there is a third person, the meeting is essentially public and each person is taking a position. Then the discussion becomes a negotiation. In private, people can be more open, more honest, and more flexible. There are some basic principles for managing these private disagreements:

- Listen—Be focused on listening to the words from the other party. Try to understand the meaning of his or her words.
- Find agreements, not disagreements—Try to achieve small agreements step by step. Show the other party that you are progressing.
- Focus on interests, not positions—Be focused on the interest from the other person and try to find some things in common.
- Size the prize—Determine the characteristics of the prize to recognize the achievements.
- Focus on facts, not opinions—Take into account the facts, not the opinions. Facts are real; be focused on those.

Good influencers win an ally not just an argument.

Publicize Agreements

When you have an agreement, make it public. This is where meetings are useful. Meetings should only be used to confirm in public the decisions that have been reached in private. This public confirmation of private deals is vital. The process of building confidence is a search for agreement. The agreement process is incremental. You are managing a series of persuasive conversations in parallel. At each stage of the conversation, you are trying to find areas of agreement that allow you to build consensus and confidence.

Summary

The daily life of a project manager is hard. It can be like swimming upstream in a headwind: dealing with politics, opposition, and conflict; making alliances; trying to make a difference while keeping day-to-day work in order. The commitment process gives a clue as to why project management is such hard work. In the commitment process you need to overcome a lot of obstacles created by the different project stakeholders, environment, and the organization. The project manager should be cautious choosing partners, although in some cases those partners are imposed by their organization. I am talking about difficulties created by company policies, procedures, and guidelines; I am talking about business issues and trends changes. The commitment process takes time and effort. At any one moment a project manager can have a dozen commitment conversations on the go with different people, and that conversation will happen intermittently over days and weeks. Keeping track of each conversation and orchestrating them so that they all reach the right conclusion at the right time is a fine art and an exhausting sport.

The commitment process may be hard work, but it is worthwhile investment. Once you have created mutual commitment, you have a platform for success. You have allies on whom you can rely. In the short term it is possible to persuade and bully people into agreement. Influencers have more ambition than persuaders. Influencers want willing and lasting commitment, whereas persuaders will settle for temporary compliance and acceptance. The commitment process separates influencers from persuaders. The following are the key points you need to remember from this chapter:

- At the heart of the commitment process is reciprocity. You should give and take at every stage.
- Building influence requires commitment, from both sides.
- If you ask for advice, ask early. Asking for advice is not just about flattering egos. It also works because you give your colleague a sense of control and influence over the outcome.
- Commitment is a two-way street, but is often treated as a one-way street. The goal of the commitment process is to achieve trusted-partner status.
- Human beings are territorial. We all mark out our spaces. We all tend to feel more comfortable in our home territory than in the alien world of a boardroom or the office of a customer or senior executive.
- The power of belonging sustains loyalty in even the most adverse conditions.
- Good influencers use the concept of self-control to induce high commitment and high performance.

Commitment Assessment

This test helps assess how committed you are to yourself. On a scale of 1 (strongly disagree) to 4 (strongly agree), select the number that comes closest to representing how true the statement is for you right now. Once you are done with all the questions, tally your final score.

QUESTION	SCORE
1. Do you take time for yourself each day?	_____
2. Do you think "selfish" is a bad word?	_____
3. Do you feel guilty saying no to your children, partner/spouse, family members, and friends?	_____
4. Does your job take priority over you and your family's needs?	_____
5. Do you make daily choices based on your priorities being honored first?	_____
6. Do you have a list of things you wish you could do or get done?	_____
7. Do you know how to make yourself a priority?	_____
8. Do you fear disappointing yourself?	_____
9. Are you ready to say yes to yourself?	_____
10. Do you believe making yourself happy first allows you to make others happy?	_____

SCORE TOTAL	MEANING
35–40	You are very committed to yourself.
25–34	You are committed but you may improve. Be conscious of your commitments.
1–24	Your level of commitment can be improved. Review the material in this book and take this test again after some time.

9

CULTIVATE YOUR
INFORMAL POWER

Power is like being a lady; if you have to tell people you are, you aren't.

Margaret Thatcher

In any project, the informal leader influences in different ways, and so is perceived differently. Of course, this influence does not only occur when the informal leader is criticizing or "kicking butt" but also happens as a result of other players seeing the commitment, level of intensity, integrity, and performance levels of an informal leader. For many project stakeholders, who is more inspiring: the project sponsor who has never managed any project; or the talented, respected, super-competent, and hardworking team member? Or even the less talented team member who gives 110%? In many cases the informal peer leader holds more influence.

I managed a project for a banking organization in Spain and the customer sponsor was the IT (information technology) manager. Although my manager was the customer sponsor interface person, I needed to talk to the customer IT manager on a weekly basis, sometimes more than once per week. It was not my role. It was my manager's role to talk to the customer IT manager, but as my manager only visited the customer once per month, I talked to the customer IT manager so frequently and supported him to make business decisions for the project. Thanks to that I gained a lot of credibility and confidence with that manager because of the amount of time we spent together, trying to take the customer project under control. My manager criticized me because I defended the customer. But I had gained enough informal power because I was the project manager, and I played the role of provider sponsor without formal authority most of the time.

Informal power is a power that is not legitimized through a written document but is agreed upon in an informal manner. The project manager has usually no formal authority so he or she needs to exert power through influencing the team members and other stakeholders. Project managers use informal power because they need to obtain good project results through others, influencing them without authority. When informal leaders are working toward achieving the same vision and goals as the formal leaders, they can take a tremendous burden from the backs of managers and formal leaders.

Informal project managers have some capabilities that more formal leaders do not, simply because they do not hold a position of designated authority. They can say things, for example, to other team members that could not be said by a person in an official management role, and their ability to influence is slightly different because informal leaders are often perceived differently than formal leaders. The formality of the job sometimes may diminish the level of fluent communication and trust between manager and team member just because of hierarchical reasons.

The informal leader who might take on this task is respected, perhaps trusted, based on his performance and relationships with the other players, while the owner is more likely to be in a leadership role due to his formal authority and power, and ability to instill fear in the players (note this is a generalization, since not all formal leaders are respected or use fear to motivate).

Here are a few bullet points to help you understand the power informal leaders have in any project in organizations:

- Not all informal leaders have intentionally gone out of their way to become informal leaders. Sometimes they emerge simply because others in the organization have great respect for them. For example, I gained the respect from other project managers when working at HP as a project manager just because of my hard work, positive attitude, vocation of service, effort, and project management internal initiatives. It took me several years of continuous project management support activities inside the organization.
- Although informal leaders can be important or even essential to the success of an organization, they can also be huge

impediments if they start pulling in directions that are in opposition to the direction the formal leader's value. For example, I
was assigned to create a project management office at HP in
Spain in the year 2000, and I did it. But I managed that project
with a lot of obstacles due to the lack of project management
maturity of my manager. I had the opportunity to influence
many people in the HP organization along that project.

- Formal leaders may want to take steps to more completely
  develop their informal leaders and keep lines of communication open with them.
- Although it may seem that promoting informal leaders to formal positions of power makes sense, it is also the case that
  some informal leaders may become ineffective if given formal
  authority (while some may be very successful). This is because
  formal authority may alter the relationships of the new formal
  leader with his or her formal peers.
- Care needs to be taken when trying to harness the power of
  informal leadership. An informal leader's power and influence
  often derives from the perception that he or she has integrity, and stands up for what he or she believes, because their
  behavior has demonstrated that. When formal leaders try to
  co-opt, or manipulate informal leaders, the risk is that the
  informal leaders will rebel or stand against the formal leader.
  Attempting to bribe, coerce, or otherwise pressure an informal leader to toe the line may end up backfiring.

The Power of the Informal

Concepts and processes that enhance productivity are often found in
informal places and in keepers of the culture. For example, we all
know that each business has a well-defined project structure, with
boxes and lines delineating who reports to whom. But we also know
that there is an informal power structure as well that is not reflected
in the boxes and lines, and people in certain positions can have much
more power than the chart implies. The same is true about getting
things done. Is it better to create sidewalks where the builders expect
the traffic to flow; or to watch the traffic flow, then build the sidewalks where the patterns emerge?

Hidden in the dusty corners of your project is a person, let's call her Rose. Every business has a Rose; in fact most business functions have a Rose. Rose is the keeper of the "How Do I" list. She knows the best way to accomplish many tasks and knows why these approaches are correct. When a new employee joins a project, if she manages to meet Rose, she will quickly learn about the informal power structure and how to get things done. The good news about these informal processes and knowledge databases is that we finally have the tools to capture and share them. Now, we aren't talking about short cuts, but about the most effective methods to obtaining information about the culture that may not be readily apparent.

If we can capture the knowledge that Rose has and publish it in the social media for more people to share, we will all be more effective. If a website can have a "Frequently Asked Questions" section, why can't a business process or a work team?

When I first started working with the "Getting Things Done" methodology, rather than create files I created piles. Then, over a period of several weeks I reorganized the piles and used those piles to create my folders. There were patterns and logic in the piles that I might not have captured at first and that became evident with a little contemplation.

What's my point? There are informal knowledge sources and "experts" in doing business in your business. Capture their knowledge and expertise and publish it for the work team or division, so that everyone can become more productive.

Informal power is obtained from your team members. That is why a good leader should remember that his informal power might not last forever. Your team members can quickly recall this privilege from you.

Four Ways to Build Your Informal Power in a Project

You know that project manager assistant who keeps the bowls of candy by her desk and always engages passersby in friendly conversation? She just might have more informal power than the company bigwig who employs her. Following are some ways to obtain informal power:

- Align your personality with the organization—Companies value project managers who fit in with the company culture. They will be more likely to have their ideas heard and win respect from senior management, regardless of title. In my experience when you manage a customer project, sometimes you are passing more time at the customer site than in your office. Because you spend much time in the customer organization you perhaps will defend more in the voice of the customer than the voice of the service provider. You need to find the balance between both parts to achieve your project objectives and be aligned with your organization.

- Know how to influence an outcome—If a decision is not yours to make, you can still fight for the results you desire. A savvy project manager knows how to order, emphasize, and withhold information when making a presentation. Some project managers, for example, place controversial project issues at the end of a long meeting, when everyone is too exhausted to put up a fight.
- Form alliances—Whether between peers or a mentor and mentee, alliances involve an exchange of support or resources that can be banked, owed, or redeemed. It is not surprising that employees with the most informal power have numerous allies throughout the organization, from interns on up to partners.
- Cultivate a reputation for power—Although this does not mean bullying your employees, it is important to create an impression that you are not afraid to use your authority. This wins respect not only from your employees but from superiors as well. All of this serves as a reminder that even when you have reached that big corner office, power within an organization is still a fluctuating thing. If you are not working on building your alliances and making your influence felt, you can be sure that others with eyes on your job are doing just that.

Project Manager Feelings

I frequently hear comments from several project managers such as:

"I am the owner! Why do I feel so powerless?"
"Why don't my team members do what I tell them?"
"I wish I had more influence with my partners."
"My team members frustrate me."

Why do project managers so often feel like this? Owners and managers are often frustrated because they fail to motivate fellow owners and employees to consistently and enthusiastically work toward project or business success.

This frustration is related to influence. The frustration can be reduced by understanding the limitations of formal power and the great potential of informal power. Influence is defined as affecting the behavior of others, in this case team members and project stakeholders. Let me illustrate with a personal experience:

Many years ago a manager from a local firm came to me after a two-day leadership workshop and stated: "I am going home to get my organization back!" Before the workshop, he had assumed that because he was the owner, he was the one his employees were following.

He had sensed that something was not right but did not know what it was. After learning about the many sources of power and considering what was happening on his organization, he recognized that a longtime employee was the one who was actually most influencing what was happening in the organization.

Informal Power

The good news is that project managers and firm owners need not always rely on formal power in working with partners, employees, and trusted advisers. They can use informal-power sources to build trust so that partners, employees, and trusted advisers will follow because they want to. A second advantage of informal power is that it is available to everyone, even if they have no formal power. You do not need a formal title to use informal power.

Informal power sources include:

- Expert power—Expert power is based on one's possession of expertise, skill, and knowledge, which, through respect, influence others. Everyone knows that you are the dairy or crop expert. That expertise brings you and your ideas great respect. You also, however, often have more education, knowledge, and experience than others at your firm in many additional areas including leadership, supervision, financial analysis, and interpersonal relationships. Use this expertise to generate great ideas. Power comes from great ideas that you are able to communicate to others.

- Reward power—Reward power is based on one's ability to reward people. Followers believe that their cooperation leads to gaining positive incentives such as recognition or promotion. Remember that behavior is most determined by consequences. Positive feedback and other nonmonetary rewards are powerful forms of power.

- Personal power—Personal power is based on one's personal traits. Personal power is your ability to influence through effective interpersonal communications. A person high in personal power is generally liked and admired by others, enabling them to influence others. A person high in personal power is often referred to as having charisma.

- Information power—Information power is based on the person's access to information that is valuable to others. This power base influences others because they need this information or want to be let in on things. Early access to financial information and to future plans is an example of information power. Managers in all fields including dairy farmers often expect employees to willingly and enthusiastically do as told because they are the boss—they have the formal power. Realistically, though, if we want to influence people to follow willingly, formal power should be the last choice. Formal power produces compliance but not willing followers. All leaders must use formal power at least on some occasions, but its use should be minimized.

Effective firm owners, like all leaders, minimize the use of formal power and instead maximize the use of informal power, especially reward, personal, and expert power. Effective leaders and managers utilize a variety of informal power to build trust and gain commitment, enthusiasm, and passion from their employees, and only resort to the use of formal power when absolutely necessary.

How to Increase Your Informal Power as a Project Manager

Here are five ways to increase your informal power and not feel you are just playing the game.

1. Know what's going on—Information is power, so be on constant alert. You need not only to know the status of the project but knowing the details talking to several people frequently.
2. Have skills, will travel—This is what you bring to the employment table. Be prepared as much as you can, you need to deal with people and overcome many obstacles during every project.
3. Develop a strong brand—It conveys your distinctiveness as a professional or leader. Use your character, use the appropriate words, you may make a difference.
4. Enhance your reputation—Toot your horn occasionally and have others do it as well. Show up daily and lead by example.
5. Build good working relationships—They are the bread of career life, so eat often and hearty. Establish, sustain, and maintain good relationships with all your project stakeholders.

Summary

I want to remind you of some key points that were explained in this chapter:

- Informal power is a power that is not legitimized through a written document but is agreed upon in an informal manner.
- Informal power is obtained from your team members. That is why a good leader should remember that his or her informal power might not last forever. Your team members can quickly recall this privilege from you.
- If you are not working on building your alliances and making your influence felt, you can be sure that others with eyes on your job are doing just that.
- The frustration of failing to motivate team members can be reduced by understanding the limitations of formal power and the great potential of informal power. Influence is defined as affecting the behavior of others, in this case team members and project stakeholders.

- Effective firm owners, like all leaders, minimize the use of formal power and instead maximize the use of informal power, especially reward, personal, and expert power.

Power Assessment

On a 7-point scale, where 1 = strongly disagree, 2 = disagree, 3 = slightly disagree, 4 = neutral (neither agree nor disagree), 5 = slightly agree, 6 = agree, and 7 = strongly agree, answer the following questions.

STATEMENT	SCORE
1. I spend a lot of time and effort at work networking with others.	_____
2. I am able to make most people feel comfortable and at ease around me.	_____
3. I am able to communicate easily and effectively with others.	_____
4. It is easy for me to develop good rapport with most people.	_____
5. I understand people very well.	_____
6. I am good at building relationships with influential people at work.	_____
7. I am particularly good at sensing the motivations and hidden agendas of others.	_____
8. When communicating with others, I try to be genuine in what I say and do.	_____
9. I have developed a large network of colleagues and associates at work who I can call on for support when I really need to get things done.	_____
10. At work, I know a lot of important people and am well connected.	_____
11. I spend a lot of time at work developing connections with others.	_____
12. I am good at getting people to like me.	_____
13. It is important that people believe I am sincere in what I say and do.	_____
14. I try to show a genuine interest in other people.	_____
15. I am good at using my connections and network to make things happen at work.	_____
16. I have good intuition and am savvy about how to present myself to others.	_____
17. I always seem to instinctively know the right things to say or do to influence others.	_____
18. I pay close attention to people's facial expressions.	_____

Add your score (the numbers you wrote after each statement) and divide by 18. You will have a score between 1 and 7. Higher scores mean you have more political skill; lower scores mean you have less. You should be above 4—and possibly well above 4—if you have aspirations to reach great heights of power.

10

UNDERSTAND HOW TO CONVERT YOUR PROJECT VISION INTO REALITY

Vision is the art of seeing what is invisible to others.

Jonathan Swift

Influence is about making things happen. It is about making great things happen that you could not achieve alone, for example, converting your idea into a real project means converting your vision into reality. Influence is about helping you make your dreams come true, to achieve more than you ever thought possible. To be influential, project managers need to make a difference and that requires ambition.

This book tries to be a practical guide to developing influence. Your project dreams and ambitions will be different. But your biggest obstacles are not about lack of money, lack of contacts, or lack of support. The biggest obstacle to success is in your own head. Here are some of the thoughts that come to my mind every time I start a new project:

- I cannot do it; it is far too big.
- If it fails, I will look really stupid to family, friends, and colleagues.
- If it is such a good idea, why has no one done it before?
- I have no idea how to start.
- I don't have the time for this.
- Other people know more about this than I do.
- Someone will steal my idea if I start talking about it.
- There are some horrible downsides and risks to this idea.

All of those objections come down to one problem: You do not really believe in yourself and your idea. You have to slay these bad ideas. Otherwise you will go into your old age always thinking about what might have been, could have been. If you do not believe in your idea you will not be able to sell your idea to someone else, so you cannot influence them.

So how do you overcome these bad ideas, short of going to a shrink every week or listening to motivational audiobooks? These are not desirable options. Put simply, you need a method. You need something that you can use in a risk-free manner while slowly building and exploring your idea. Your idea may be you want to win over a stakeholder or motivate your team. Whichever it is, I propose you a simple method that I call IRM (idea, resources, and money).

With IRM, you don't need to be courageous and take huge risks in pursuit of your dream. IRM follows the principle of incremental commitment: you build your dream step by step. If you find that there is a fatal flaw in your idea, IRM allows you to exit gracefully and fight another day.

It may seem that you need courage to chase your dream, and I discovered that courage is important but not enough. Well-trained people who will get the job done are necessary.

The IRM (Idea, Resources, and Money) Principle

In my professional experience, each successful idea has followed the same pattern: idea, resources, and money (IRM) while being converted into a project. And they come in that order. Any idea may be converted into a project trying to influence people, for example, selling the idea, looking for resources, and being funded.

The Idea

Always start with the idea: a good idea will attract great people, attract the investment, and eventually make money. The bigger the idea, the better: it is easier to attract people and investment to a big idea than it is to a small idea. People usually will be influenced by great ideas. The issue is how to discover the great one.

Telling people to have a good idea is like telling them to be witty and inspirational. It is not easy. So how do you have a good idea? Fortunately, there are a number of tried and tested ways of coming up with winning ideas, as follows.

1. Copy an idea
2. Solve a problem
3. Listen to your customers, suppliers, and partners

Hopefully, you now have several great ideas for your organization. But how do you know that they really are great? How do you know that they are not fatally flawed? A little bit of desk research will quickly weed out the worst ideas. But do not disappear into a darkened room for months doing research on your idea. There is a better way of developing it. Talk to people. Ask questions to your customers. For instance, when I started the "Project Portfolio Days" project it was based on a survey I ran with my customers about their interest in project portfolio management. I researched the market and at that time no similar international event had been organized in Spain. So I made a lot of customer visits and tried to get my customers influenced by the idea for more than six months. We tried to influence our customers by adding value for them. I failed the first year but tried again and was successful in the second year. Sixty people attended the event. It was a very successful project.

Talking to people greatly accelerates your idea. By talking about it, you will achieve three things. You will:

1. Find out any flaws in the idea fast
2. Develop your idea fast
3. Find out who you want on your team, and find backers and supporters for your idea

Usually, people have two sorts of objections to sharing their idea with other people. First, they are worried that other people will steal their idea. There is always that risk. But in practice, other people have their own lives to lead. They are busy chasing their own dreams and fighting their own fires. Your idea may be entertaining and exciting, but they will not have the energy and passion to develop the idea and pull together the team. They will happily jump on your bandwagon, but stealing your bandwagon is too much effort. When I launched my idea of the Project Portfolio Days event I was not only influencing my customers but also my market competitors. They could copy my idea, and by being first I took the risk. I believed in my project and finally I made it happen.

The second objection is that they will look stupid when they share the idea: this is the classic fear of rejection. You can overcome this by using the PASSION principle (see Chapter 1) for the structured conversation. You no longer have to sell your idea; instead you gently explore the idea with a potential partner. Use the PASSION principle well, and your partner will be explaining to you how your idea can work, rather than you explaining it to them.

And finally, be bold with your idea. The bolder it is, the more likely you are to make progress. If you have an idea for reducing the amount of paper clips in the office, that is worthy but will be ignored. The bigger the idea, the more people will be interested, and potentially excited. When developing the Project Portfolio Days idea, I had the opportunity to visit a lot of C-level directors and I took advantage of that. If in doubt, be bold.

Human Resources

Venture capitalists rarely back just a great idea. They normally also back a great team. An average idea from a great team is more likely to succeed than a brilliant idea from a weak manager. This is not just how venture capitalists think. It is also how senior managers in your organization are likely to think as well. They back people even more than they back ideas.

In most of the ventures I have started, I have had no relevant credibility, experience, or contacts. So the solution is simple. If you lack personal authority and credibility, borrow credibility from someone else (it is one of the best practices of using influence). Find people with credibility, influence, and authority who will support your idea. And this is where you need to dance a little. Do not expect powerful and busy people to drop everything and put their reputations on the line to support you. That will not happen.

Again, go back to the principle of incremental commitment. Ask for a small "give." When we started Teach First, we knew we could not get big companies to immediately fund us. Instead, we simply asked them if they would sign a pledge that said Teach First was a good idea. Most businesses were delighted to be let off so lightly: they all signed. Soon enough we were able to produce brochures that showed that we had the support of many of the top businesses in the United

Kingdom. That created confidence and gave us legitimacy. Suddenly, government ministers were willing to talk to us and other top businesses wanted to be associated with us. The bandwagon started to roll.

Within your own organization, you can follow a similar approach. Don't ask for everything all at once. Ask finance to sign off on the financial side of things. Do not ask finance to evaluate the whole idea, because it may raise other concerns. If that is too much to ask, then get finance to evaluate the possible benefits of your idea, without any of the costs. You then have a prize to dangle in front of everyone else, a prize that is worth fighting for. Do the same with other departments: ask for partial approval of one aspect of the idea. Build your coalition slowly. Keep any disagreements in private; do not let opposition become public because then it becomes hard to shift. But make sure any partial agreements are widely publicized. Build your bandwagon of support, so that success seems inevitable. Keep your doubts to yourself.

You need the right people to support you. With each of these people, use the principles of influence to engage them. As you talk to them, you will find they naturally select themselves. Some select themselves as potential team members, others deselect themselves. And it is very obvious which are which. The main difference is how they deal with problems. Even enthusiasts may see problems with your idea, but they will immediately start searching for solutions. They are the people you want on your team. Then there are the cynics who revel in finding problems and ooze condescension and superiority. Count them out of your potential team. The right team for you is not just about skills. You also need a team with the right values. As one CEO put it: "I hire most people for their technical skills and fire most for their values." You can train skills, but you cannot train values. Make sure that whoever you enlist to support you shares your values and beliefs.

Money

If you have a great idea and a great team, the money will follow. If the money does not follow, look again at the quality of your idea and your team. The chances are that something is missing. This sounds like it trivializes the money challenge. And to some extent it does. Every start-up goes through at least one or two near-death experiences and they are usually to do with lack of money. When I was sent to run a business in Japan, I found a business with no sales, no prospect of any sales, and no existing customers. And it had a lot of bills that could be not paid. It was dead in the water. But most of the team was good, and it had a good business idea. It survived.

There is no simple formula for finding the money. A business start-up is different from a charity, which is different from finding funding within your own organization. But there are some principles to follow:

1. Size the prize
2. Build your coalition of support
3. Use the principles of influence to build support
4. Remember that no is always a prelude to a yes

The most common situation I found was to be rejected. Do not get emotional, do not get upset. That is the way things are. Learn from the rejections by asking why. It is the most important part of the story; you need to learn in order to improve the next time.

Have a Plan B

You need to be flexible and you always need a plan B. In practice, that means you should go into every meeting knowing your desired outcome, and with a backup. Whatever the outcome, there should be some next steps. Even if your idea is rejected, you should understand why. And then ask directly, "Let's meet again when we have dealt with your concerns fully." If you leave the meeting without a next step, it is very hard to build any momentum again.

Plan B means you should have alternative routes to success. If one person does not help, know at least one or two other people who could help instead. Once you become dependent on one person, your risk goes through the roof. You become a slave, not a partner, to the persons you depend on. It is a very uncomfortable position to be in.

Crisis and Opportunities

We have assumed that you are chasing a "green field" dream: an idea that is completely new and original, at least in the context of where you are working. These ideas are often exciting, but they are difficult to put into practice. By definition, a new idea is one that no one is working on, there is no budget for it, and no one supports it to start with. Your new idea will create extra work, require extra resources, and cut across existing agendas and priorities. And most people are risk averse, which means that they see new ideas as risky; they will upset the existing way of doing things. No wonder it is hard to build support for a new idea.

Fortunately, you do not need to have a brilliant new idea or leave your organization to stake your claim to fame. In most organizations, there is a constant stream of opportunities for you to stake your claim to fame. Occasionally, the opportunity is presented gift wrapped for you. Beware of such gifts: the gift may be less attractive than the wrapping. I was gifted the opportunity to take a one-way ticket to Japan where our business was in chaos. Or perhaps you are offered the opportunity to take on a "challenging" budget or new business opportunity. "Challenging" is business speak for mission impossible.

More often, your opportunity will come carefully disguised as a crisis. Fortunately, organizations are crisis prone: suppliers let you down, the competition messed you up, customers want everything by yesterday, key staff disappear, and genuine crises blow up out of nowhere. These can be perfect opportunities to stake your claim to fame.

There is always a moment, at the start of each crisis, where no one is quite sure what to do. No one knows who should take the lead. Some colleagues will be denying that there is a problem; others will be busily trying to figure out who should take the blame if things get really ugly. This is the moment of uncertainty when the real leaders emerge: they take control and lead the way to a solution. Offer to sort out the problem and your bosses and colleagues will be relieved. It will be one less thing for them to worry about. The bigger the problem, the more opportunity you have to make a name for yourself. Crisis accelerates your career. You will succeed fast or you will fail fast. You will achieve visibility to top management well beyond daily responsibilities. It pays to know how to deal with crises well.

Let's start with how not to deal with crises:

- Deny the problem—Crises do not sort themselves out. They have a habit of getting uglier all the time.

- Find someone to blame—Passing the buck may help your short-term survival, but it creates a poisonous fog of politics and ensures you acquire enemies for the future.
- Get angry, frustrated, or depressed—You will be judged as much on how you are as what you do. And emotions are infections: if you start getting angry or frustrated, others will follow you. That is not productive.

It may seem obvious that these are ineffective ways of dealing with crises. They also happen to be very common ways in which people react to crises. Even when a pitfall is obvious, people still fall into the pit.

How you can deal with a crisis well:

- Recognize the problem early—The sooner you deal with it, the easier it is to sort out.
- Take control—Offer solutions, not problems. Have a plan. Or at least, build a plan fast with your colleagues.
- Focus on what you can do—Build momentum, build confidence. There may be only one small thing you can do (call an emergency meeting, for instance). If that is the only thing you can do, then do it. Do not worry about things you cannot control, because you cannot control them.
- Find support—Find people who can help. Don't try to be a lone hero. There are more people who may help you in your organization.
- Overcommunicate—There will be fear, uncertainty, and doubt. Be clear and consistent; have a simple story to tell about what you will do.
- Be positive—You will be remembered as much for how you behaved as for what you did. Be the role model for others to follow. Wear the mask of confidence and purpose, even if you feel doubt and fear behind your mask.
- Avoid blame—Leave that to the postmortem. Create a culture of action and cooperation, not analysis and blame.
- Be generous—Do not hog the credit, be lavish in your praise of everyone who helps. By giving praise, you are also showing that you were in control and taking the lead.

Summary

Influence is not an end in itself. It is a means to an end. Only you can decide what you want to achieve. But in case of doubt, be ambitious. Most of us are limited not by our ability but by our ambition. Ambition for your company, your team, and yourself is good. When you are ambitious you set an agenda that resonates across the organization, not just in your own silo. In this sense, influence is like your credit card. Once you go beyond your formal limit of credit and you can cope with it, you get invited to extend your credit even further. Bigger and larger opportunities come your way.

To be ambitious as a project manager means

- Be firm about the goals, flexible about the means
- Support and enable the team at all points
- Give the team a sense of control
- Read the warning signals

To be influential, project managers need to make a difference and that requires ambition.

Vision Assessment

Assess your own readiness for creating and implementing a workable vision for your team. For each statement, determine if the statement is in place, partially in place, or not in place and place an "X" in the corresponding cell.

STATEMENT	IN PLACE	PARTIALLY IN PLACE	NOT IN PLACE
Your vision is the foundation for high expectations.			
The vision is a vital part of performance assessment.			
Your vision is in an ongoing state of evolving.			
You work to motivate the team to close the gap between your vision and reality.			
Your vision pushes professional assumptions.			
Your team uses your vision as a basis for assessing the organization.			

STATEMENT	IN PLACE	PARTIALLY IN PLACE	NOT IN PLACE
The professional staff has translated your vision into concrete action.			
Your professional staff has a clear understanding of what the vision means in educational practice.			
The staff uses your vision as a measure of professionalism.			
Your vision is regularly revisited and modified as circumstances change.			
Your professional staff has committed to the vision.			
Your vision provides a common language for professionalism.			
The professional staff was a vital part of the vision's development.			
New staff members are made aware of the organization's vision.			
The community supports your vision.			
As a leader, you serve as a promoter and guardian of the vision.			
You remain patient as staff members take their time to meaningfully embrace the vision.			
You encourage a culture that allows for growth and change.			
You provide professional development to support the spirit and intent of your vision.			
You celebrate advances toward your vision.			

PART II

SELL YOUR HORSE

11

DEVELOP AND SUSTAIN
YOUR INFLUENCE

Example is not the main thing in influencing others. It is the only thing.

Albert Schweitzer

To develop and sustain your influence is a critical success factor in my experience. Like most other practices it needs to be "sold." Individuals fulfilling the role of the project manager need to sell their horse; they need to sell the features, advantages, and benefits of a particular idea or project, but they also need continuous feedback on how they are doing.

The project manager adds value to the organization positively influencing project stakeholders to obtain project success. The point is how to tell the project management story to the rest of project stakeholders. I suggest to identify and to emphasize the few key competences of project management that can transform organizations. My suggestion is to tell stories, to try to translate the message into a story that is easily understood.

Selling to different project stakeholders the need for project management in your organization is one of the most important steps in implementing organizational project management practices. I have talked to project managers around the globe and we believe that to gain the go decision from executives you must follow the three-step selling model that I call EPF (evaluate, prepare a plan, and follow). This method to gain project stakeholders buy-in is the result of the experience of project managers on the field who have successfully implemented project management in organizations gaining the support from their executives.

The Selling Model

This selling model is broken into the following steps also shown in Figure 11.1:

1. Evaluate—Understanding the needs of the project stakeholder you want to influence.
   1.1 Understand the need. The best way to cover the stakeholder needs is to understand the key strategic priorities for the organization. Understand their strategic priorities, goals, and objectives, and see where your project is and how important it is for your organization.
   1.2 Evaluate your environment. Then you must select a stakeholder who will be most affected by the benefits and value produced by the project.
   1.3 Is he or she the right person to influence? If this same individual was also responsible for troubled projects from the past it will even be easier to gain his or her support when you can relate back to those projects and explain how a strong relationship between the project stakeholder and you as a project manager can produce a big business impact.
   1.4 Share your thoughts with other peers and colleagues, and always speak about the project and its business impact, not about you as a project manager. Ask the management team for consensus about getting a sponsor assigned to your project.

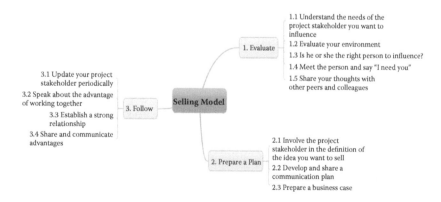

Figure 11.1   The selling model.

2. Prepare a plan

   2.1 Involve your project stakeholder from the beginning, and talk about his or her expectations and your expectations. Remark how the project stakeholder can help the project manager and his or her team to achieve a big business impact throughout that project. Brainstorm about what, how, and when the project stakeholder will be necessary, and his or her interaction with the project manager.

   2.2 Develop and share a communication plan. Communication with business leaders and those in need of project management is often forgotten. The organization must be informed about the value and capabilities of project management and the willingness of your group to help the business units meet their goals.

   The plan must include the target audience, frequency and type of information presented, issues to be mitigated, the escalation process, progress updates, capabilities, and benefits. Advertise, advertise, and communicate.

   2.3 Prepare a business case. A business case must be completed with all key business unit personnel. Producing the business case as a team will help to get buy-in from all departments involved and the upper managers. This business case will be your selling tool for gaining funding approval.

   The business case must include:
   - Key business challenges, goals, and objectives you want to address
   - Proposed sponsorship strategy; your approach, your expectations, and project resources
   - Benefits and value project sponsorship will bring to the organization
   - Proposed cost
   - Rollout plan

   The secret to selling a project stakeholder is to focus on his or her primary business need and the value that he or she can bring the organization. The primary business needs come from the first step (understanding the need).

3. Follow—Talk to your project stakeholder frequently. Keep him or her informed about the project. Help him or her to

understand that working together we will know much more about the project, then he or she will be much more valuable for the organization.

The Right Assignment

The path of leadership is often a random walk of experience. With good bosses and projects we learn and grow fast. And then we find a boss from the dark side and the project from hell. Suddenly survival is success. If we are to build our careers and our influence, then we have to have the right boss, with the right project in the right organization. Finding this magic combination is our responsibility. If we leave our career direction to the tender mercies of the human resources department, then we have to hope to get lucky. But hope is not a method and luck is not a strategy. If you delegate your career to human resources, you will discover that "career" is both a noun and a verb. When you let others take control, career becomes a verb that accurately describes your random walk to the future. When you take control, your career will move forward. I love the following quote from Mahatma Gandhi: "Take care of your thoughts because they will become your words. Take care of your words because they will become your facts. Take care of your facts because they will become your habits. Take care of your habits because they will become your destiny."

I want to share with you three simple tests to determine if you have made the right choice of boss, firm, and project, when you can afford it:

- Will I learn and have the right experience?
- Will I succeed?
- Will I enjoy it?

Having the Right Experience

In theory we need to learn from schools, training courses, textbooks, and lectures. In practice, project managers learn from experience. We see someone mess up and quietly make a note not to do the same thing. We see someone do something very well and might try it ourselves. Books and courses tell us what we need to do; experience shows what actually works. Then it is your most crucial tool.

The key experience test is to ask yourself: What skills will I need to flourish one or two levels further ahead in my career? That means you need to learn new things, rather than become ever more expert at your current job. Expertise may be well paid, but it is not the high road to the top. As your career progresses, technical skills become decreasingly important. Instead, people and political skills become essential; the subtle arts of influence become more important to further your progress in an organization. In practice, this requires gaining experience of working across the organization, not just within your own department. You have to push beyond your comfort zone. As you deal with other departments, you have to deploy influencing, political, and people skills in abundance. By definition, you cannot tell other departments what to do—you have to influence and persuade them. Let me share with you my experience in an information technology (IT) project as a project manager when I worked for Fujitsu in Spain:

Fujitsu won a project in a bank in Spain. The project was an infrastructure project to install several computers in the different Spanish locations (Madrid, Valencia, Barcelona, Seville, Bilbao, Palma de Mallorca, and Tenerife), with customized software for the bank. Then the participation from several departments of Fujitsu was needed. I prepared a project plan and I shared my project plan with all the project stakeholders. The project management culture from Fujitsu was low in Spain. Then nobody gave me any criticism about the project plan. I asked them one by one about their project commitment and they said yes. However, the authority that my company conferred me was low. The bosses from the software department, support engineering, and sales considered me a technical guy, not a project manager. At the moment the project started, and I asked for some resources at every computer installation, I needed to wait because those resources were not available. When I complained to the management team, I was told that my project was generating a lot of work load, my project had many issues, that I was always asking for resources for my project, and so on.

I needed to call a meeting with management. I told them: Dear managers, it is not my project; it is a customer project that Fujitsu won. I need your collaboration in the benefit of the project success and the Fujitsu success. I cannot be successful without your collaboration. I am supposed to be the project manager, in charge of this project of course. But I need your cooperation and support. I want you and your people working on the team with me and I respect your obligations and responsibilities.

That meeting started changing the behavior from some managers. The good results, I mean their cooperation and collaboration, were not immediate, but I planted some seeds that soon produced some fresh fruit.

Being Successful

There are some questions to ask:

- Will I have the right team?
- Will I have the right budget?
- Will I have achievable goals?
- Will I have a supportive boss?
- Do I have the right skills?

It pays to play hardball before you accept the project. The moment you accept the project, all your negotiating power has disappeared. Playing hardball can be done constructively. No one wants an assignment to be set up to fail: your negotiation should be about how to set the project up for success. Everyone should want a positive outcome. Keep pushing until you are satisfied. You do not need to have changed the entire team before you start, but you need to make sure you have the right to change it fast after you start.

The success question leads to a huge trap. You need courage to stretch yourself. So the extra success question you should ask is: Will any success be noticed at least two levels above me? If only your boss knows of your success, then you are invisible and that is not a good way to build influence or to lay a claim to fame.

By focusing on success that is visible across the organization, you stretch yourself and you force yourself to earn the skills that you will need for the future.

Enjoy What You Do

I have yet to meet a CEO who does not enjoy what he or she does. Of course many CEOs are professional complainers: they grumble about all the traveling they have to do, the taxes they pay, and the burdens they have to bear. That is their way of boasting about how much they travel, how much they earn, and how important they are. They grumble and love every moment of it. Equally, I know of no athlete or artist who dislikes what he or she does, despite the endless hours of tedious practice. Put simply, you only excel at what you enjoy. The project management career is a marathon, and it has plenty of bleak and challenging moments. Anyone can sustain enthusiasm for a day or two. You have to find something you genuinely enjoy doing.

There is a trap with this question. Most people do not leave their organization; they leave their boss. But the corporate carousel keeps on turning. A bad boss today can be replaced by a better boss tomorrow. As a rule, it is better to seek a move within your organization than to jump to another organization. The new organization will put its best face on when trying to recruit you and you may like your new boss. You then move and find that your new organization still has politics, crises, and incompetence; and your new boss may have been replaced by a boss from hell. When headhunters promise you greener pastures elsewhere, remember that it is greenest where it rains most. Or you may make the decision to start a new company.

Finding the right assignment is easier said than done. It starts by finding the right employer. If you join a traditional firm that downsizes every two years, it is harder to progress than if you join a start-up that is growing at 50% per year. But the start-up may also go bust next year. So your starting point is to judge your prospective employer as much as they judge you. Only work for a firm that has a source of unfair advantage. The problem with a fair fight is that you might lose it. The only fights worth having in the market are so unfair that you are bound to succeed.

When I worked for HP as a project manager, I always tried to find the right project. I made some friends in human resources. And I kept my ear to the ground. I made myself useful to bosses at least two levels above: when they have good opportunities, they will keep you in mind. When some projects fail, management looks for victims. Make sure you are very busy and very committed elsewhere. When the golden opportunity starts to emerge, make yourself available: offer to put in some voluntary help to get things going, to help the boss. Make yourself part of the new opportunity. Be a risk taker but be careful. Control your destiny, or someone else will.

Taking over a New Team or Role

Influence and power are closely linked. Influence is about creating informal power that extends beyond your formal authority. Power comes from your formal position, in theory. But in practice, there are many people in positions of power who are not in control. The classic example is when your project team needs to work on the customer site over the weekend and you as a project manager are at home, not in power. You can have the title but still not have the power, unless you use it.

The first rule of power is use it or lose it. That means taking over properly from day one. Within a month of taking over, everyone on your team, and your colleagues and your bosses will have decided what you are like in your new role. Changing those initial perceptions is hard work. Your agenda for taking over successfully is the same as the agenda for making your dreams come true. It is the IPM (idea, people, and money) agenda. And this is how the agenda works when you take over.

Having an Idea

If we want to be grand, we can call this your vision. But it is no more than your story of what you are going to do in your new role. Your story will have three parts:

1. This is where we are.
2. This is where we are going.
3. This is how we will get there.

If it takes you more than ten seconds to say where you are going, that is too long. The whole story need not be more than 30 seconds. No one will remember the long, sophisticated analysis and 37-point plan that you dream up with your consultants. And if they cannot remember it, they cannot act on it.

A good idea can be very simple, such as:

- We will focus on customer service.
- We will improve time to market.
- We will achieve best-in-class costs.
- We will professionalize the project work packages.

From one simple statement, a whole battery of initiatives can flow. Your one simple idea can focus on the organization, give it direction and purpose, and clarify priorities. Without a simple idea, you will have confusion in your head and in your team. And if you want to make your vision or idea motivational, make it relevant to each member of your team. Show how they can help achieve the vision you have laid out. If you decide that you want a customer-focused organization, then clearly both the receptionist and the toilet cleaner have an important role to play: they make an impression on customers. Once you have your idea, you need to sell it.

People

Never assume that the team you inherit is the team you have to live with. It will be a mix of the good, the bad, and the ugly. Like any sports coach, one of your key tasks is to build the right team. Some of that comes through training and developing your team; some of it comes from making sure each member of your team is in the right position; much of it comes from bringing the right people into the team from the start.

Expect to restructure your team within a month or so of taking over. If nothing else, this is a good way of showing you are in charge. One new boss of a large IT division found herself in charge of eight geographically based power barons who liked to think that they were kings of Italy, France, Germany, Spain, and so on. Within a month she had reorganized around industries. The reorganization in theory was about building expertise. In truth, it was an exercise in power. All the power barons were moved into industry sectors, and a couple lost their jobs. Suddenly she was the all-powerful queen of the business and the barons were cowed into obedience. The old ritual execution has a powerful effect on the survivors. Previously she had not been in control of the barons; within a month everyone knew who the boss was.

Reorganizing is a wonderful way to reset the psychological contract with each member of your team. It is a chance to sit down with each one and explain exactly what you expect. Expectations are not just about performance goals; they are also about the way of working. That makes the discussion a two-way street: they need to hear what you expect and you need to hear what they expect. If you can listen and act on what you hear, you are likely to build respect and loyalty fast.

Having the Money

Your predecessor may well have left you a few postdated checks, which you will be expected to honor. He or she may have painted a picture of a unit that is on the brink of success where efficiency and profits will soar. If you live with that, you will live with hell.

You need to reset expectations very fast. Search all the cupboards for all the skeletons that have been hidden. Paint a picture of a unit that is near to total collapse. It is going to take a genius (you) to prevent catastrophe occurring. If your version of events is accepted, then survival is success. Set expectations low and overdeliver.

Expectations of performance and budget are, or should be, linked. Fight hard for the budget you need. When you take over, there will be plenty of things to distract you. You will be learning all about your new unit and your new team; you will be learning new skills; you will find yourself sucked into a new routine of reporting and meeting; there will be fires to fight and deadlines to meet. This day-to-day survival can be completely overwhelming when you first start in a new role. Do not get sucked into the frenzy of day-to-day activity. Delegate everything you can to your team; see how they cope. Give yourself time to build your IPM agenda, gain support for it, and then act on it. It is the investment of time that will ensure you set yourself up for success.

Budgets   In theory the budget process is a rational method of allocating resources efficiently across the organization. In practice, the budget process is very political. It is the process where each level of management negotiates a contract with the levels above and below. The goals of the negotiation are the mirror opposite of each other depending on your position. When negotiating a budget with your bosses you should seek to minimize your promises and maximize the resources you are allocated. When setting a budget for teams beneath you, you need to do the opposite: maximize the promises you get and minimize the resources you have to commit.

If you want a year of living in hell, try being macho and accept the "challenging" budget you are first presented with. All managers should rise to a challenge, in theory. But they should not sign up to a year of chasing lunatic goals with minimal resource. Ensuring that you have the right budget settlement follows the same principles as influencing any sort of decision. Influencing decisions is clearly a key task of any influencer. For our purposes now, it is enough to note that the budget is a must-fight and must-win battle of the annual corporate calendar. Do not leave it to the planners and finance department to seal your fate for the coming year.

Influencing Decisions

A project is not a democracy. Decisions are made which affect you and your career, but you do not get to vote on those decisions. That does not mean you cannot influence those vital decisions, such as budgets, assignments, team allocation, priorities, and more. If you are to have any influence as a project manager, you have to know how to influence decisions in your favor.

There are nine principles that practicing project managers can put to use (see also Figure 11.2):

1. Anchoring—Should my project budget be cut by 5% or 10%? I don't know, but the debate has just been anchored around a cut and the compromise may be around a 7% cut. If you don't like that, then make sure that you anchor the debate for your sponsor around whether your project can have its budget increased by 15% or 20%. Stake your claim first.
2. Framing—I asked my partners if they would like to invest 500,000 euros in building a profitable business in Dubai, and avoid the cost of supporting my business trips to the Gulf region. They agreed, which meant that they agreed to losses of 500,000 euros in three years. I supposed that if I had asked

Figure 11.2   How to influence decisions.

if I could lose or waste 500,000 euros of their money, they would not have been so supportive. Investment is good and "losses" are bad, even if they are the same thing. Your words make the difference.

3. Loss aversion—Would you invest your pension fund in a policy that offers an 80% chance of doubling your money, but a 20% chance of losing it all? If you could play that game often enough, perhaps you would win. But because you can play only once, most people would duck the offer, because the risk of loss is too great. When asking for a decision to be made, understand the potential losses and risks for the other person. If you eliminate the risk, you will eliminate the opposition.

4. Social proof—Informally build a coalition in private, one-on-one meetings, keeping conflict private and making agreement public. Endorsement from senior managers counts, but also make sure you gain the support of finance and all the other functions who cannot say yes but have unlimited authority.

5. Emotional credibility—We believe what we experience more than we read. Do not rely on data and facts alone to make your case. Bring your case to life with example stories.

6. Restricted choices—What happens when we have several choices is that making a decision will be much more difficult, and we will leave confused. The more choices you offer, the greater the risk you create. I mean you create the risk in

the buyer's mind that they made the wrong choice. Restrict choice; make it easy for people to say yes.

7. Repetition works—Be persistent, I mean that if you repeatedly stake your claim, eventually even the most absurd nonsense can become the received wisdom.

8. Idleness—Your peers, team members, or managers may like you and your idea, but they probably do not like it enough to drop everything they are doing to help you out. So make it easy for them, ask them for the minimum required. Eliminate any administrative or logistical hurdles for them.

9. Size the prize—Focus on the benefits of your idea. Doing anything is risky, but doing nothing is a huge risk.

Meetings

I had a manager in a multinational firm who loved meetings: "They are a great opportunity to sabotage the agendas of other colleagues." Meetings serve many different purposes, not all of which are about sabotage. But whatever the meeting is, you need to have your own agenda. If you work to someone else's agenda, that is very noble. But if you want to make progress and build influence, you need to know each meeting can help you with your priorities and agenda.

A successful meeting will answer one or possibly all three of the following questions:

1. What did I contribute? A good way of building influence is having a positive attitude. Have a look through the formal agenda beforehand to see what and where you can contribute.

2. What did I learn? Every meeting can be used as a learning opportunity. You may learn about what is happening in a project, learn about politics, or learn how other people handle themselves well or poorly.

3. What did I achieve? You need to have cleared what you want to achieve. Perhaps you will find the most productive part of the meeting is just before the meeting, just after, and in the coffee break. That moment is where you can have informal conversation with hard-to-get executives. If you need a formal decision, you need to obtain it at a meeting, do not leave it to chance.

If you cannot positively answer each question, the meeting has been a waste of time and you should not have attended.

Presentations

Death by a hundred bullet points to the head is an ugly way to go. But this is the fate that too many presenters inflict on their audiences. These set pieces are where you can achieve great visibility. No one will have seen all your weeks of late nights, but they will see the presentation. These are the moments when you accelerate to success or failure: at promotion time, the bosses will remember your presentation and will have no idea about all the hard work that you put in beforehand. Understandably, many people become nervous about making formal presentations. Presentations are a mixture of style and substance.

Style wins. Try to remember a presentation you watched from a year ago; you probably cannot remember much of the substance. But you probably can remember the style of the presenter, for better or for worse. First we will look at style and then at substance.

Style

If you can manage your enthusiasm, your energy, and your excitement presenting (the three E's), you are likely to do well. If you do not project those emotions into the audience, no one will be enthusiastic, excited, and energetic for you. You need to lead by example. As an experiment, try explaining the tax implications of your firm's transfer pricing policy to some friends. Chances are you will not sound very interesting to them. Now try recounting the most exciting legal and decent thing you have done in the last year. Chances are that you will naturally display the three E's. Everyone has the natural ability to display the right style. You simply need to transfer your natural ability into the business environment.

To help you transfer the three E's to the stage, visualize what success looks like. If you can, go to the venue beforehand under the guise of checking the logistics. Then make sure you know exactly how and where you will stand; and how you will work the slides, if any. Imagine yourself looking and sounding confident and succeeding. Rehearse success in your mind, and then go and do it.

Substance

If a presentation is important, do it well. That means preparing and rehearsing. Here is how to set yourself up to succeed:

1. Have a clear goal—Even if the presentation is simply to report on progress, you should have in mind what a good outcome looks like. Then organize your presentation to achieving that outcome. And when you start your presentation, make sure your audience knows what the purpose of your presentation is. It is very important to be clear about what they should expect.

2. Tell a story—Telling a story is important. You don't need to be creative. Tell a real story, something you lived and experienced, something significant.

3. Keep it short—A presentation is not complete when you can say no more. It is complete when you can say no less. Focus on what is most important. This is where your story is essential: have a clear, simple story around which you can hang the key evidence you should provide.

4. Dumb slides, smart presenter—Use as few slides as possible. Do not fill your slides with a lot of figures and numbers. Concentrate in the message you want to get across the audience.

5. Support assertions with facts—You need to support your messages with concrete facts.

6. Present for the audience, not for yourself—Work out who you are presenting to. If you are presenting to 50 people, there are probably just one or two people you really need to influence. Focus the presentation on those two people. This will give your presentation structure, simplicity, and focus, which the other 48 people will appreciate as well.

7. Start well, end well—I script the first 30 seconds of what I will say. However nervous I may feel, the script lets me start confidently and engage the audience. And I have a standard finish for all presentations, which leaves people on a high, rather than the limp "Any questions?" Script your finish as well as your start.

8. Get it right—One bad number destroys the credibility of the whole presentation: it invites a shooting gallery where

everyone is looking for the next error. Equally, spelling errors show a lack of professionalism and reliability.

9. Focus, focus, focus—Focus your story to make it simple; focus your message on the people you need to influence; focus your eyes on each individual in the audience. Do not talk to your slides. Talk to the audience.

10. Prepare, prepare, and prepare—The more you prepare and rehearse, the more confident you will be.

Conflicts

Organizations are set up for conflict. So seeing projects as temporary organizations they are set up for conflict, too. Conflicts are part of everyday life. Inevitably, different functions have different views of what is important.

Different business and geographic units think their own area is most important, and they are competing intensely with each other for the same limited pot of investment. Internal competition is the way in which resources are allocated across the organization. And this conflict is explicit in multinationals that invite bids from national subsidiaries for the location of the next manufacturing plant or research and development center. And of course, all staff members compete with one another for the same limited pool of promotions and bonuses. The real competition is not in the marketplace; it is sitting at the desk near you.

Most of the time, it pays to compete collaboratively: create win–win situations. This is the art of influence. But occasionally, you need to stand your ground. You need to know when to fight and when to compromise. Fortunately, Sun Tzu gives us the answer. Over 2,500 years ago he wrote *The Art of War*. He laid out three conditions that needed to be fulfilled before going to war. These conditions are as true of today's corporate battles as they were in ancient times:

1. Only fight when there is a prize worth fighting for.
2. Only fight when you know that you will win.
3. Only fight when there is no other way of achieving your goals.

Only Fight When There Is a Prize Worth Fighting For

Many corporate battles fail this simple test. The end result of such battles is a loss of trust all around, which is a poor way to build influence. But there are a few battles where there is a prize worth fighting for:

- Budgets
- Assignments
- Team formation

The price of losing, or worse not even fighting these battles, is very high. To succeed, you need the right role with the right budget and the right team. Do not compromise.

Only Fight When You Know That You Will Win

Generals like to say that most battles are won and lost before the first shot is fired. The same is true of corporate battles. If you have lined up not just all the arguments but also all the people in support of your position, then you will win. If you are not sure that you will win, then the chances are that you will lose. The saying on Wall Street holds true for any organization: if you don't know who the fall guy is, you are the fall guy. If you properly line up all the support beforehand, then any rational opposition will melt away before any conflict erupts.

Only Fight When There Is No Other Way of Achieving Your Goals

As a rule, it is better to win a friend than to win an argument. You may think you have gloriously routed all your enemies in a famous victory. Rest assured that you have enemies. They may or may not accept that they have lost the battle, but they certainly will not think they have lost the war. They will bide their time. And in the way the corporate world goes, colleagues and even team members can become your boss, or become people on whom you depend heavily. If you get to the point where a bare-knuckle fight is the only way of achieving your goals, then something has gone seriously wrong with your preparation and influencing skills.

Summary

To develop and sustain your influence is a critical success factor for your project success as a project manager, so let me summarize the key points to remember:

- The project manager adds value to the organization positively influencing project stakeholders to obtain project success.
- The secret to selling a project stakeholder is to focus on his or her primary business need and the value that he or she can bring the organization.
- By focusing on success that is visible across the organization, you stretch yourself and you force yourself to earn the skills that you will need for the future.
- Put simply, you only excel at what you enjoy. The project management career is a marathon, and it has plenty of bleak and challenging moments. Anyone can sustain enthusiasm for a day or two. You have to find something you genuinely enjoy doing.
- The first rule of power is use it or lose it. That means taking over properly from day one. Within a month of taking over, everyone on your team, and your colleagues and your bosses will have decided what you are like in your new role.
- Never assume that the team you inherit is the team you have to live with. It will be a mix of the good, the bad, and the ugly.
- If you are to have any influence as a project manager, you have to know how to influence decisions in your favor.
- Presentations are a mixture of style and substance. Style wins. Try to remember a presentation you watched from a year ago, you probably cannot remember much of the substance.
- You need to know when to fight and when to compromise.

Getting Buy-In and Making It Happen

Building a buy-in strategy can take time and effort, but most successful programs are based on just a few key steps.

KEY STEP	DESCRIPTION
1. Make your goal clear.	People have trouble achieving vague visions, so it helps to set a clear objective. You might try a quantitative approach, such as cutting landfill waste by 30%. Or you might take a more qualitative tack, such as eliminating every possible ounce of landfill waste. Either approach can work if you follow the next steps.
2. Ask why it is hard.	Conducting a survey can tell you a lot about people's attitudes toward the goal and the barriers they encounter. Some barriers make compliance virtually impossible, such as a lack of recycling bins. You'll need to remove those barriers first. Other barriers might have more to do with perceptions, so you will need to address those next.
3. Use a personal touch.	E-mails and memos are easy to ignore, but people are not. So you should ask people to commit to the program in person. The old adage about catching more flies with honey applies here: Coercion usually fails to get results.
4. Seek public commitments.	Your goal is to create new social expectations among your coworkers, and the best way to do this is to ask for commitments from groups of people. Try to involve everyone, so nobody can remain passive. This will help people see themselves as environmentally conscious and on the team. Whenever possible get them to sign up in writing— and do it in public—because written commitments are stronger than verbal ones. Getting commitments is a very big step, but many people will have difficulty staying on track, especially at first. The next step is to help people stick with the program until it becomes a habit.
5. Use prompts.	Reminders help, especially when they are easy to see and understand. Pictograms and simple words work best. Put them where you want people to make a change, such as above wastebaskets or recycling bins, in the copy room, or wherever you want people to change their behavior. Encouraging messages empower people, while negative messages tend to turn them off.
6. Remind people of new norms.	Many factories have big banners reminding workers about the importance of safety and doing high-quality work. Reminding people about the company's sustainability goals is equally important.
7. Talk about progress.	Acknowledging progress and talking about challenges and barriers is an ongoing part of building new norms. Over several weeks or months, your positive program will begin taking on a life of its own.

We tend to think about our positive goals, but the art and science of changing behavior is an equally important piece of the puzzle. This outline can get you started on the right path.

PART III
RIDE YOUR HORSE

12

THE MYTHS OF INFLUENCING

The first myth of management is that it exists. The second myth of management is that success equals skill.

Robert Heller

If you have developed your influencing skills to become a project manager of influence, finally *you must ride your horse*. I mean you need to put in practice all the influence skills you have developed so far, take action, and face the potential and real issues you may find as a project manager. You need to answer the question: Are you well prepared to influence or not? Now you need to be effective and efficient influencing the different project stakeholders. Are you ready to do it? Unless you try it you will not know it. Test it and see what happens. Gaining good influence skills is not an overnight process; it takes time, effort, and patience. And for sure you will fail at the beginning; nobody is perfect. Along my career I made many mistakes when trying to influence my team members, executives, peers, and colleagues. I faced many difficult situations having the need to influence people in the projects I managed in my whole professional life. I guess I was not prepared enough and I failed. But my attitude was always to learn from my mistakes, and I made many mistakes in my project manager life. Ride your horse and observe if your horse is under control, that is use your influence skills and verify if you are being successful. Perhaps you need to tune up your influence skills. Learn from it and take action again, and again, and again. If you still fail, try it again because it is not the end. Be persistent!

Our society has created some myths about influence that affects our way moving forward to influence team members and other project stakeholders in the project we manage. This chapter is a collection of some experiences gathered from colleagues regarding the myths of influencing; I hope to be practical and useful for you.

Mistakes and Myths

According to the research of Gregory Schrempp, Indiana University (see the Mythology Studies program at Indiana University), a myth "refers to colorful stories that tell about the origins of humans and the cosmos" (Mary Magoulick). Attitudes toward myth vary greatly. Some regard it as a source of spiritual growth, while others see only falsehood. Some see in myth the distinct character of particular cultures, while others see universal patterns.

The subjects of influence and power are shrouded in mystery and much misunderstood. Project managers are comfortable learning about things like planning and control. But learning about influence and power sounds devious, divisive, and self-interested. This is unfortunate, because influence and power are central to making organizations and projects work. As years go by, many project managers become more aware of the importance of soft-skills development. A project manager needs to influence without having authority over different project stakeholders. So project managers need to develop their soft skills and be ready to learn from anybody on a project. I like the sentence: "You can be my teacher." Everybody can learn from anybody else.

Main Mistakes

The foundation of influence is trust. Most project managers forgive most misdeeds. They know that mistakes happen and disasters occur. They can forgive bad jokes, bad dress, and occasionally bad judgment. The one thing most bosses find unforgivable is breach of trust. Once a project manager no longer trusts a team member, it is game over. It may take weeks or months, but eventually the project manager and team member will part company. Equally, few team members want to work with a project manager they do not trust, even if they like the project manager personally. Peers have a choice about whom they collaborate with: Trust plays a central part in that choice.

Lack of Trust

Without trust it becomes very hard to build alliances, commitment, and support across the firm. There is much more to being an effective influencer than trust, but lack of trust is a killer. Breaking trust is not just a matter of undermining a colleague or a project manager. It also includes bad-mouthing people behind their backs; breaking perceived promises and commitments, not being honest, or misleading people; and failing to support an ally or a project manager at a critical moment. All of these are betrayals. Even if what you did was technically correct, the sense of betrayal will remain. Shattered trust is like shattered glass: it is very hard to rebuild.

For example, when leading a project management office (PMO) at a multinational company in Spain, the project sponsor from one of the projects running in the organization talked to me behind the back of the project manager. He was unhappy with the performance of that project manager and instead of talking to him directly, facing the issue, and practicing trust, he was talking behind his back to different managers in the organization. This situation demonstrated a lack of trust on the project manager from the executive. When that project manager knew about it he felt frustrated.

It is impossible to have a close relationship when people do not trust their partners, peers, or team members. Trust involves knowing that a partner has your best interest at heart. It is hard to feel safe and secure when you are involved with someone who would betray your trust. Not only is trust important, but it also influences our deceptive behavior. People have a fundamental need to get even; it is called "reciprocity." And reciprocity is one of the most studied aspects of our human nature. We like to treat people as we have been treated. Smile at someone and watch what happens back. This desire to reciprocate—the desire to return favors and repay punishments—is very difficult to control. So when a partner betrays our trust, it is natural to want to get even. Essentially people think "If you are not honest with me, why should I be honest with you?" And reciprocity helps explain why trust is so important in a relationship. If you do not trust someone, who you are close to, you are less inclined to tell the truth. Deception can quickly take over a relationship when trust is missing.

The Influence Myths

The art of influence and power is not Machiavellian politics. Plotting against colleagues, stabbing people in the back, and being devious is not the way to gain power and influence. Effective influence is based on trust. There is a calculating element to influence: you have to know where and when to invest precious time and effort building your alliances. There is also a ruthless element to influence: knowing when to seize the moment and take control of an agenda. This kind of calculation and ruthlessness is a benign force for the individual and the firm. Everyone benefits when you make the right investments and manage the right agenda. Influence is not, however, about being nice.

Influence is not about being liked or making friends. Influence is based on alliances of common interests and trust. Eventually, a professional alliance may become a personal friendship.

When creating my first PMO in Madrid I needed to find some allies for the project. So I asked to participate in some sales and support meetings. That way I knew much better the measures and objectives from these departments that participated actively in every project of that organization. I established and maintained a personal relationship with them during the whole PMO project. However, it was not a path of roses for me all the time. I found some resistance in some departments that did not like my approach and they felt threatened in their job position and functions because of my PMO project. But when the project finished and the PMO was operating I counted on some friends, not all of them from these departments, because I also had some adversaries. My friends supported me in my efforts; they influenced the rest of the organization speaking positively about the efforts that my team and I were doing establishing a PMO. They overcame some obstacles about project management awareness in my department, but they supported me all the time. Finally everybody in the whole organization obtained some benefits and advantages of the PMO creation.

The goal is to create a productive alliance, not to make a personal friendship. The friendship myth is important because it is natural for people to seek popularity. This simply leads to weakness, pandering to other people's demands, and dancing to whatever the mood music of the day might be. Influential relationships are based on partnerships, not friendships. Partners act as equals: they work toward common goals and hopefully share a common understanding of how things should work.

Some people see influence as evil and manipulative; some want influence to have morals and to be a force for good. Influence does not have morals. It is neither moral nor immoral: it is amoral. It is a force for good or a force for evil, depending on who uses it and for what purposes. In other words, influence is as moral as the person who uses the skills of influence. Hopefully you use influence as a force for good, and knowing how influence works you will better resist influence when it is in the wrong hands. That is your choice.

Successful influencers seem to have a magic about them. Everyone wants to get a piece of their magic pixie dust. Like charisma, influence is treated as something you either have or do not have. Because effective influencing is invisible to third parties, it appears to be even more magical and mysterious. The simple message of how to influence and persuade is that there is no magic to influence; or if there is, this book has decoded the spell. In place of magic there is a series of skills, behaviors, and mind-sets that all managers can acquire to become influential. As you build these skills you will slowly master the invisible art of influence.

Colleagues wonder how you make things happen so easily, how you seem to find the right opportunities, how you turn crises into opportunities, and why so many people help you. Whether you share the secret of your magic is for you to decide. Based on my professional experience I have recognized some myths about influence in managing projects in organizations:

- Myth 1: Be pushy, overbearing, and intimidating
- Myth 2: Use bribes to make people do what you want
- Myth 3: Pay for a service in order to get something you want
- Myth 4: Perform an influencing role such as a priest, a teacher, or a policeman

Myth 1

Some people believe that by being pushy and intimidating they can exert more influence and get better results. I can share with you my personal experience with an executive when serving as a project manager for a service provider organization: I worked as a project manager for an external customer and obtained good project results and good customer satisfaction over the duration of the project. The relationship with my manager was good and I shared some personal and family issues with him from time to time believing he was a trustworthy person. Then I was promoted as manager of project managers acquiring the same management level he had. He talked behind my back to the rest of the managers telling them that I would not be effective enough because I had some personal issues to solve. He tried to intimidate me on several occasions until I escalated the problem to the human resources department. He broke our trusting relationship. Since that moment I never shared with him any other personal experience or story.

Myth 2

Some people believe that everybody has a price, and they try to bribe you offering something in exchange. Let me give you an example: In a software development project in which I was the project manager, a third-party manager who collaborated with us treated me to dinner several times asking me not to say the truth to the customer about his bad team performance. My reaction was as follows: Instead of achieving his objective, I escalated that problem to my manager and his team was immediately fired.

Myth 3

Pay for a service in order to get something you want to achieve. I managed a project in which an outsourced company gave me a paycheck just for helping them on being accepted for the next phase of the project. The manager from that subcontractor was very clear and concrete in prompting me to accept that money. I considered that an unethical action, so instead of influencing me and obtaining the desired results, they were fired as soon as I escalated the issue to my manager.

Myth 4

A role of authority such as a priest, a teacher, or a policeman carries influence. Not everybody listens to a priest, teacher, or policeman just because of the authority they represent. Although that may differ by culture, it does not always work that way. You first need to build a trusting relationship, which builds up your credibility.

Monitor and Control Your Horse

Sometimes you may receive some feedback from some project stakeholder. Other times you may observe the lack of good results yourself. When you ride your horse, that is, when you are applying your influence skills, you will see if you are prepared enough, and then you need to make a decision about spending more time developing your influence skills and learn from experience. In my experience as a project manager, developing soft skills has been the hardest part. However, the more experience you gain as a project manager, the ability to influence will be one of the most crucial soft skills you need to develop.

Summary

The following are some lessons learned from this chapter:

- If you have developed your influencing skills to become a project manager of influence, finally *you must ride your horse*. You need to put in practice all the influence skills you have developed so far, take action, and face the potential and real issues you may find as a project manager.
- Project management is about dealing with people. Influencing people is not easy but it is not impossible. You need to apply your influence skills, and perhaps you will fail more than one time. Be patient and try to learn from your mistakes. Repetition is the key.
- Once a project manager no longer trusts a team member, the game is over. Lack of trust will destroy your relationships. Project managers need to deal with and influence different project stakeholders in different scenarios. Carefully assess your stakeholders and try to act with authenticity (say what you believe) and with integrity (act on what you say). That way you will keep on your trusted relationships as a project manager.

- The art of influence and power is not about Machiavellian politics. Plotting against colleagues, stabbing people in the back, and being devious is not the way to gain power and influence.
- Be careful about the myths of influencing. Be yourself and practice honesty, hard work, and communication with all your project stakeholders. You not only need to establish and develop relationships with your project stakeholders, but you also need to sustain them.
- Monitor and control your influence skills through assessing them. Ask for help when needed from your executives, customers, and other project stakeholders. Receiving feedback is valuable for your professional success as a project manager.

13

Summary and Conclusions

If you are here now reading this chapter it is because I influenced you in some way to finish this book. Congratulations! You are the best. The purpose of this book was to help you develop your influencing skills.

People help if they owe you for something you did in the past to advance their goals. I observed that some people I supported in the Project Management Institute (PMI) are very ready to help me when I ask them for a favor. That is the rule of reciprocity. Get in the habit of helping people out, and do not wave it away when people thank you. Do not say "Oh, no big deal." Say something like, "Of course; it is what partners do for each other." In that way you arc labeling what happen an act of partnership. In that way you, as a project manager, have significantly elevated the probability of success.

In this book I have shared with you my experiences regarding how to prepare a persuasive conversation with a determined structure. I talked about the classic mistakes and how to overcome them:

- Persuading the wrong person—You do a brilliant job and gain agreement, but find later that the person you are talking to is not the real decision maker. The solution is to do your homework. You need to find out some information about the person you will meet before meeting him or her.
- Leaving without next steps—This can happen even after a brilliant meeting where everything has gone well, but you forget to state exactly what happens next. It is then very awkward to go back a few days later and try to re-create the enthusiasm that existed before. And if things have not gone as planned, you always need a plan B, which should at least involve a follow-up conversation. Solution: Know the outcome you want, and ask for it.

- Falling in love with your own idea—You talk too much and talk over the other person who will not love your baby as much as you do. In fact, they may just see a noisy mess and will object to your baby. Listening is better than talking. Solution: Ask smart questions, don't make smart comments. Failing that, buy duct tape and put it over your mouth.
- Becoming defensive: When people object to your idea, it is easy to start arguing back. Then you just have an argument. It is better to win a friend than to win an argument. Solution: Agree with the objection. Let them talk about their concerns. Ask them for advice on how they would solve their concern. Often they will solve their own problem.
- Not following up—When you have an agreement, you need to reinforce it and confirm it. Otherwise, nothing will happen. Solution: Send an e-mail immediately after the meeting thanking them for their great help and summarizing the main conclusions and next steps. After some days, phone the person to follow it up.
- Having only one plan—This is fine when things go well. But we have to deal with human nature. The unexpected happens. You need to prepare for all eventualities and to be flexible. Solution: Have a plan B, have an alternative.
- Hiding behind PowerPoint—That tool is a disaster for persuaders. It makes you talk, not listen. It gives you no flexibility. It outs the other person in the role of judge and jury and that is a role they will enjoy more than you, because you are the defendant they are judging.

In Chapter 2, I shared my best practices on active listening:

- Open and purposeful questions—When we first meet someone, it is very tempting to tell them who we are. It is part of our human nature to puff ourselves up a little. We want to make a great impression and show that we are someone who is worth talking to.
- Reinforcement—Go to your local coffee shop and watch people gossip. You may be able to persuade your boss that this is not just a break from work: it will help your work. First, observe the body language.

- Paraphrasing—If you want to show your understanding and building agreement, paraphrasing is a useful way. It is simply a summary of what someone has said to you, expressed in your own words.
- Contradiction—Contradiction is another principle of effective listening. Contradiction is not about arguing with people. It is about letting people show off.
- Disclosure—I believe disclosure is a subtle art. It can be badly done. At social events it is common to spot two alpha males fighting like rutting stags.

I also used Chapter 3 to explain the importance of developing trust to be a project manager of influence and how crucial it is for project success. Building trust in relationships with customers, team members, and project stakeholders is an essential skill for all members of a project team. In that chapter I talked about the need of building your professional credibility to better influence others. Building credibility takes a lot of time but it is worthwhile.

Integrity principles and practice were shared in Chapter 4. Saying what you believe and acting on what you say will allow you to practice authenticity and integrity. You need to practice your integrity to be a complete project manager (Randall L. Englund and Alfonso Bucero, *The Complete Project Manager*, 2012). You need to learn how to measure your integrity and to be a project manager of integrity. Measure your integrity by answering the following questions:

- How well do I treat people from whom I can gain nothing?
- Am I transparent with others?
- Do I role-play based on the person(s) I'm with?
- Am I the same person when I am in the spotlight as I am when I am alone?
- Do I quickly admit wrongdoing without being pressed to do so?
- Do I put other people ahead of my personal agenda?
- Do I have an unchanging standard for moral decisions or do circumstances determine my choices?
- Do I make difficult decisions, even when they have a personal cost attached to them?
- When I have something to say about people, do I talk to them or about them?

- Am I accountable to at least one other person for what I think, say, and do?

In Chapter 5 I shared some ideas and best practices about getting prepared in order to influence to win:

1. Look at the future—Many companies avoid team building because of past experiences that have left employees jaded and cynical.
2. Become a leader—You must use your strengths (whatever they are) to bring out the best in others. You need to focus only on your strengths and stop focusing on weaknesses.
3. Inspire people
    - Commitment—It is necessary that you live the mission and expect the whole team to follow your example.
    - Cooperation—The whole must become greater than the sum of the parts.
    - Communication—Provide all necessary information, and let the team members know that it is OK to ask for information and to share data with each other, fellow workers, and sometimes even customers.
    - Contribution—Participation is not optional in a team-work situation. You must require and support it.
4. Encourage your team—People do exactly what you reward them for doing. They don't respond to promises, requests, cries, screams, threats, or kindness. They respond to action. Reward the individual members and the team for the results you really want, and only for the results you really want.
5. Be a difference maker—Every member and the team as a whole need to feel that they are making a difference in the lives of others. Take care of the details. Always smile and empower your people.
6. Communicate the results—Teams need to feel a sense of accomplishment; they need to see the end result of a project. You need to share the results with the people involved.
7. Allow your people time for training—You must provide training for the team members and the leaders because it is a necessary ingredient for team success. Allow training on any topic that the team wants (regardless of whether it is job

related), using videotapes, audiotapes, seminars, books, and professional trainers.

8. Offer them a challenge—Everyone has limits. But how will your team members ever know what their limits are if you never give them a project that is more difficult than they thought they could accomplish? They need to learn and grow, to develop and improve.

9. Empower the team—Give full control to the team: responsibility, authority, and accountability. This means full delegation. Don't look over members' shoulders, don't question their expenses, and don't ask them to explain every decision and every action.

10. Be respectful—When they rise to the challenge and accomplish something truly outstanding, you must show your appreciation for their efforts, and reward the team accordingly.

Practicing your generosity was explained on Chapter 6. Let me share with you a personal example: When I worked for Hewlett-Packard as a senior project manager I liked to offer junior project managers my help in terms of giving them some advice and dedicating some time to talk to them periodically. I was perceived by my mentees as a valuable professional, but my manager said that I diverted a lot of time and effort to my colleagues' problems. You also had the opportunity to assess your generosity using the assessment provided in that chapter.

After reading Chapter 7 you should have understood the importance of understanding the different styles of people, their major issues and problems, and how to deal with them.

You need to understand people, but remember that:

1. Everybody wants to be somebody—There is not a person in the world who does not have the desire to be someone, to have significance.

2. Nobody cares how much you know until he or she knows how much you care—If you want to be a project manager with influence you need to love people before you try to lead them. The moment people know that you care for and about them, the way they feel about you changes.

3. Everybody needs somebody—Everybody needs friendship, encouragement, and help. What people can accomplish by themselves is nothing compared to their potential when working with others. Doing things with other people tends to bring contentment.

4. Everybody can be somebody—Once you understand people and believe in them, they really can become somebody. And it does not take much effort to help other people feel important. Little things, done deliberately at the right time, can make a big difference.

5. Anybody who helps somebody influences a lot of people— The final thing you need to understand about people is that when you help one person, you are really impacting a lot of other people.

How to develop commitment was dealt with in Chapter 8. Influence is about encouraging people to keep on doing something and to keep on supporting you. Building influence requires commitment from both sides. I shared in the chapter my best practice of asking for advice and its consequences.

My experiences and ideas about informal power were explained in Chapter 9. Informal leaders have some capabilities that more formal leaders do not, simply because they do not hold a position of designated authority. I suggested some ways to build your informal power at work and how to increase your informal power:

1. Align your personality with the organization—Companies value project managers who fit in with the company culture.

2. Know how to influence an outcome—If a decision is not yours to make, you can still fight for the results you desire.

3. Form alliances—Whether between peers or a mentor and mentee, alliances involve an exchange of support or resources that can be banked, owed, or redeemed.

4. Cultivate a reputation for power: While this doesn't mean bullying your employees, it is important to create an impression that you're not afraid to use your authority.

A power assessment in that chapter compared formal and informal power.

I talked about how to convert your vision into reality in Chapter 10, how to convert your dreams into a real project. I also provided a vision assessment. A good idea will attract great people, attract the investment, and eventually make money. The bigger the idea, the better: it is easier to attract people and investment to a big idea than it is to a small idea. People usually will be influenced by great ideas. The issue is how to discover the great one. Telling people to have a good idea is like telling them to be witty and inspirational. It is not easy.

Developing and sustaining your influence is the subject of Chapter 11. To develop and sustain your influence is a critical success factor in my experience. I talked about selling and obtaining buy-in from executives, using the following selling method:

1. Evaluate—Understanding the needs of the project stakeholder you want to influence
    1.1 Understand the need
    1.2 Evaluate your environment
    1.3 Is he or she the right person to influence?
    1.4 Share your thoughts with other peers and colleagues
2. Prepare a plan
    2.1 Involve your project stakeholder from the beginning
    2.2 Develop and share a communication plan
    2.3 Prepare a business case
3. Follow—Talk to your project stakeholder frequently

And in Chapter 12 I explained the influence myths that I found and the potential mistakes you can make as a project manager.

The foundation of influence is trust. Most project managers forgive most misdeeds. They know that mistakes happen and disasters occur. They can forgive bad jokes, bad dress, and occasionally bad judgment. The one thing most bosses find unforgivable is breach of trust. Once a project manager no longer trusts a team member, it is game over.

Without trust it becomes very hard to build alliances, commitment, and support across the firm. There is much more to being an effective influencer than trust, but lack of trust is a killer. Breaking trust is not just a matter of undermining a colleague or a project manager.

Finally I would like to remind you of the six principles of persuasion that Robert Cialdini identified in his book *Influence:*

- Liking—If people like you they are more apt to say yes to you. But you need to be careful that being likable does not become a detriment. People will take advantage of that for their own benefit.
- Reciprocity—People tend to return favors. If you help people, they will help you. If you behave in a certain way, they will respond in kind. My personal approach is to be a giver because the return will come, perhaps when you do not expect it.
- Social proof—People will do things they see other people doing, especially if those people seem similar to them. We cannot avoid belonging to our society and following some practices that are normal.
- Commitment and consistency—People want to be consistent or at least to appear to be. Ask yourself if you are really committed. Commitment and consistency are very linked.
- Authority—People defer to experts and to those in positions of authority.
- Scarcity—People value things more if they perceive them to be scarce.

I strongly believe that influence is an art. When I was in high school, I had a swimming coach who loved motivational quotes like: "Quitters never win, and winners never quit." Those sentences helped me to maintain a good performance as a swimmer and were imprinted in my mind over the years. As a project manager you are a leader. Leadership is not just about having a powerful position. Anytime you use your influence to affect the thoughts and actions of your project team members and stakeholders, you are engaging in leadership. The best leaders are those who understand that their power flows through them, not from them.

Based on my project management experience I have some best practices to suggest that may help you to be an influential project manager:

1. The key to influencing people is to catch them doing something right. When you discover that your team members have done something right, tell them they did a great job, recognize them.
2. Be proactive and do not wait until your people do things exactly right before you praise them.

3. Be focused on the full part of the bottle. Be positive and recognize small achievements from your people.
4. You will obtain from people what you expect. You need to clarify your expectations to your team members and be patient, being always positive and hopeful with your people.
5. People who produce good results feel good about themselves. Help people to feel good when they achieve something tangible and encourage them.
6. Feedback leads to great achievers. You need to give feedback to your people.
7. No one can make you feel inferior without your permission. You decide if today is a good day or a bad day for you. Always choose a positive attitude.
8. No one of us is as smart as all of us.
9. Get your ego out of the way and move on. You are a leader who needs to serve your people.

I really hope that reading this book gave you some insights that may positively affect your career. Enjoy your journey. Today is a good day!

Bibliography

Bolman, Lee G., and Deal, Terrence E. (1997). *Reframing Organizations*. San Francisco: Jossey-Bass.

Bucero, Alfonso. (2005). Getting senior executives to buy into project methods: A case study. PMI EMEA Proceedings, Edinburgh, Scotland, May.

Bucero, Alfonso. (2010). *Today Is a Good Day: Attitudes for Achieving Project Success*. Ontario: Multimedia Publications.

Bucero, Alfonso. (2011). Your words, as a project manager, make a difference. Proceedings of the PMI Global Congress 2011—EMEA, Dublin, Ireland.

Bucero, Alfonso. (2013). Sell the horse: How to develop your influence skills for project success. PMI EMEA Congress, Istanbul.

Cialdini, Robert B. (2000). *Influence Science and Practice*. 4th ed. New York: Pearson, Allyn, & Bacon.

Covey, Stephen R. (1990). *Principle-Centered Leadership*. New York: Free Press.

Englund, Randall, and Bucero, Alfonso. (2006). *Project Sponsorship: Achieving Management Commitment for Project Success*. San Francisco: Jossey-Bass.

Englund, Randall, and Bucero, Alfonso. (2012). *The Complete Project Manager: Integrating, People, Organizational, and Technical Skills*. Tysons Corner, VA: Management Concepts.

Englund, Randall, and Bucero, Alfonso. (2013). Develop your personal skills to be a complete project manager. Proceedings of PMI Global Congress 2013, Istanbul, Turkey.

Frame, J. Davidson. (1999). *Building Project Management Competence*. San Francisco: Jossey-Bass.

Goleman, Daniel, Boyatzis, Richard, and McKee, Annie. (2002). *Primal Leadership. Realizing the Power of Emotional Intelligence*. Boston: Harvard Business School Press.

Graham, Robert J., and Englund, Randall L. (2004). *Creating an Environment for Successful Projects*. 2nd ed. San Francisco: Jossey-Bass.

Juli, Thomas. (2010). *Leadership Principles for Project Success*. New York: CRC Press.

Kerzner, Harold. (2010). *Project Management Best Practices: Achieving Global Excellence*. 2nd ed. Hoboken, NJ: Wiley.

Moran, Robert T., Harris, Philip R., and Moran, Sarah V. (2007). *Managing Cultural Differences*. 7th ed. Burlington, MA: Butterworth-Heinemann.

Pinto, Jeffrey K. (1996). *Power and Politics in Project Management*. Newton Square, PA: Project Management Institute.

Index